PRE Get Up To Speed 02

PRE GET UP TO SPEED 2
Focuses on a wide range of daily situations
providing learners with the opportunity to deal with and improve
their proficiency and confidence in communicative English.

CARROT HOUSE

Pre Get Up To Speed 2
© Carrot House

All rights reserved. No part of this publication may be reproduced,
stored in a retrieval system, or transmitted in any form or by any means
without the prior permission in writing of Carrot House

Printed: May 2021

Author: Carrot Language Lab

ISBN 978-89-6732-142-0

Carrot Global Inc.
9F, 488, Gangnam St., Gangnam-gu, Seoul, 06120, South Korea

Curriculum Map

Course	Level 1	Level 2	Level 3	Level 4	Level 5	Level 6	Level 7
General Conversation	Essential English : Begin Again; Pre Get Up to Speed 1~2; Daily Focused English 1	New Get Up to Speed+ 1~2; Daily Focused English 2	New Get Up to Speed+ 1~2; New Get Up to Speed+ 3~4	New Get Up to Speed+ 3~4; New Get Up to Speed+ 5~6	New Get Up to Speed+ 5~6; New Get Up to Speed+ 7~8	New Get Up to Speed+ 7~8	
Discussion			Active Discussion 1	Active Discussion 1; Active Discussion 2; Chicken Soup Course; Dynamic Information & Digital Technology	Active Discussion 2; Dynamic Discussion; Chicken Soup Course; Dynamic Information & Digital Technology	Dynamic Discussion; Chicken Soup Course; Dynamic Information & Digital Technology	
Business Conversation	Pre Business Basics 1	Pre Business Basics 1; Pre Business Basics 2	Pre Business Basics 2; Business Basics 1	Business Basics 1; Business Basics 2	Business Basics 2; Business Practice 1	Business Practice 1; Business Practice 2	Business Practice 2
Global Biz Workshop				Effective Business Writing Skills (Workbook); Effective Presentation Skills (Workbook)	Effective Business Writing Skills (Workbook); Effective Presentation Skills (Workbook); Effective Negotiation Skills (Workbook); Cross-Cultural Training 1~2 (Workbook); Leadership Training Course (Workbook)	Effective Negotiation Skills (Workbook); Cross-Cultural Training 1~2 (Workbook); Leadership Training Course (Workbook)	
Business Skills			Simple & Clear Technical Writing Skills	Simple & Clear Technical Writing Skills; Effective Business Writing Skills; Effective Meeting Skills; Business Communication (Negotiation); Effective Presentation Skills	Effective Business Writing Skills; Effective Meeting Skills; Business Communication (Negotiation); Effective Presentation Skills; Marketing 1; Management	Marketing 1; Marketing 2; Management	Marketing 2
On the Job English			Armed forces 1; Armed forces 2; Aviation 1; Aviation 2; English for Cabin Crew; English for Call Centers; English for Medical Professionals	Armed forces 1; Armed forces 2; Aviation 1; Aviation 2; English for Cabin Crew; English for Call Centers; English for Medical Professionals; English for Aviation Maintenance Technicians	English for Aviation Maintenance Technicians		

※ This Curriculum Map illustrates the entire line-up of textbooks at CARROT HOUSE.

CARROT HOUSE

PRE GET UP TO SPEED 2

Introduction

Carrot House Methodology

Andragogical Approach & Productive English

The teaching of children (pedagogy) and adult learning (andragogy) are distinctively different. Pedagogy is akin to training and encourages convergent thinking and rote learning. It is compulsory, centered on the teacher and the imparting of information with minimal control by the learner. Andragogy, by contrast, is about education as freedom. It encourages divergent thinking and active learning. It is voluntary, learner oriented, and opens up vistas for continuing learning. Adults need to feel independent and in control of their learning. Therefore, Carrot House curriculum is based on andragogy and is designed to encourage learners' participation and engagement by providing more task-based activities and opportunities to frequently interact in the classroom.

People want to achieve communicative competence when they learn other languages. English education in EFL environments has been rather focused on the receptive skills of English—listening and reading—which simply increases learners' knowledge about a language, not the competence of using it. If people are well equipped with productive skills—speaking and writing—they will be competent in English communication.

This is why Carrot House curriculum is designed to enhance learners' productive skills throughout the course. This andragogical approach of the Carrot House Curriculum, which focuses on productive English, will enable learners to achieve communication skills necessary for global competence. Carrot House's teaching philosophy and curriculum combine to provide a "Language for Success" for all learners.

Communicative Language Learning (CLL)

This communicative interaction, the essential component of language acquisition, does not occur in a typical, non-meaningful, fun-oriented conversation with native speakers. It occurs in a negotiated interaction through which a well-trained teacher provides the comprehensible input that is appropriate to the learners. The learners, at the same time, actively utilize the opportunities given to them by the teachers.

To this end, the Communicative Language Learning (CLL) method is employed in the field of Foreign Language Acquisition. The CLL method provides activities that are geared toward using language pragmatically, authentically, and functionally with the intention of achieving meaningful purposes.

Course Overview

Objectives

PRE GET UP TO SPEED Course Book series are designed to improve proficiency and enhance the confidence of learners' communicative English in the areas of listening, speaking, and comprehension. The Books focus on a wide range of topics to provide learners with the opportunity to deal with language and themes that a native speaker would face on a daily basis.

Lesson Composition

Pre Get Up To Speed 2 consists of 16 lessons and 8 review activities. Each lesson consists of 9 sections.

1. Getting Started

This two part activity is designed to stimulate the learner's thinking through picture description and situation related questions, and put them at ease in an English speaking environment.

PRE GET UP TO SPEED 2

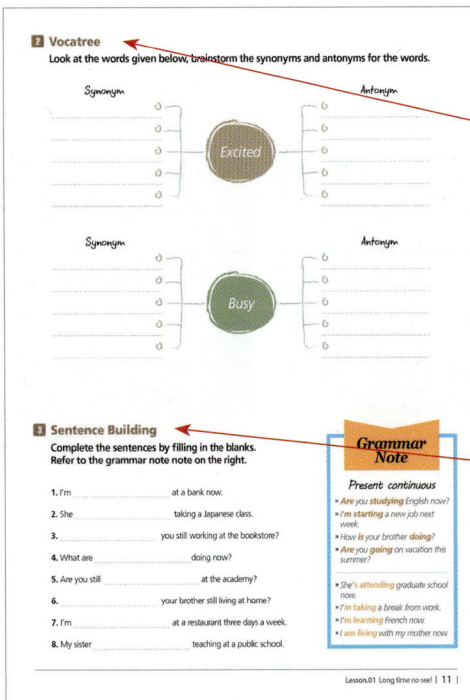

2. Vocatree

Gives learners the chance to expand their vocabulary through brainstorming the synonyms and antonyms of key vocabulary.

3. Sentence Building

Provides an overview of the grammar used in each lesson along with a sentence building activity to practice the lesson's grammar.

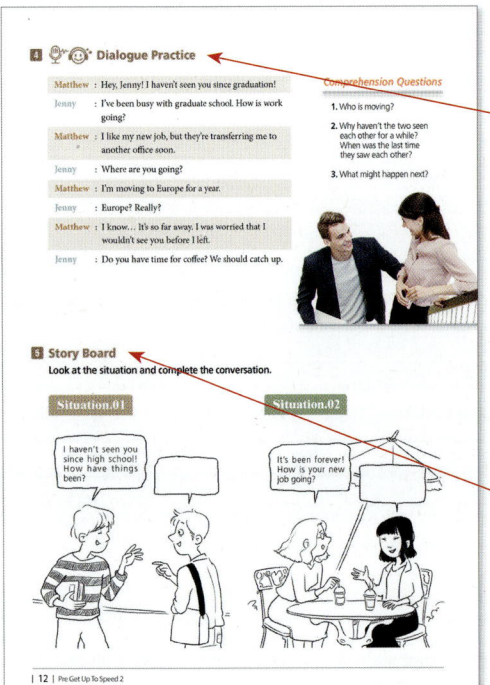

4. Dialogue Practice

This section provides a conversation based on the topic of the lesson which includes the key language patterns for learners to practice and understand native English speaking style. Audio scripts and Mp3 files provided.

5. Story Board

Uses visual materials describing two different situations for learners to practice the language patterns of the lesson.

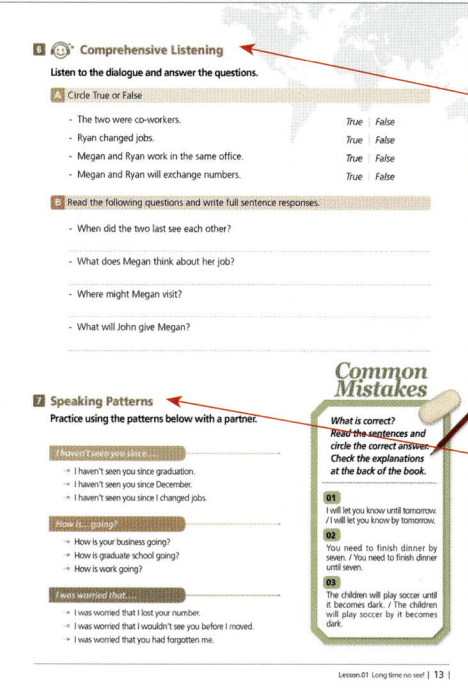

6. Comprehensive Listening

Extended dialogues and questions to provided learners with an area to expand on their listening and comprehension skills. Audio scripts and Mp3 files provided.

7. Speaking Patterns

Acts as a practice ground for reinforcing topic based useful daily expressions and patterns through substitution drills.

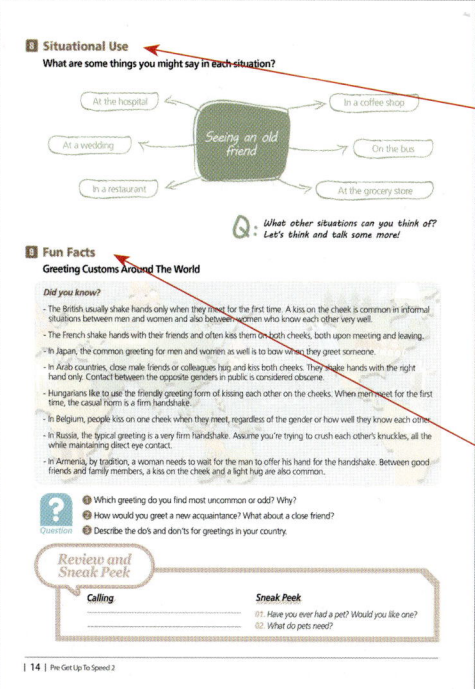

8. Situational Use

Topic guided speaking practice for learners to utilize the language patterns and grammar learned in each lesson.

9. Fun Facts

Presents interesting facts for learners to reflect upon and express their own opinions.

CONTENTS

Unit.01

Lesson Title	Learning Objectives	Speaking Practice	Grammar Note	Page
Lesson.01 **Long time no see!**	- greet old friends and acquaintances - use the present continuous to discuss activities you are currently engaged in	· I haven't seen you since…. · How is…going? · I was worried that….	Present continuous	10
Lesson.02 **I'm walking my pet**	- discuss household pets - use verbs of necessity to talk about pets' needs	· I…twice a day. · I need to…before we go out. · Would you…my dog for me?	Necessities	15
» Review 01				

Unit.02

Lesson Title	Learning Objectives	Speaking Practice	Grammar Note	Page
Lesson.03 **Going grocery shopping**	- learn to ask for prices and describe groceries - use intensifiers and superlative adjectives to discuss different products	· These (This)…look(s) very fresh. · How much for…? · Could you give me…?	Intensifiers & Superlative adjectives	21
Lesson.04 **Healthy eating**	- talk about healthy eating habits - use adverbs of frequency to discuss healthy eating habits	· …is (are) good for… · You should eat… servings of…a day. · Too much…is not good for you.	Adverbs of frequency	26
» Review 02				

Unit.03

Lesson Title	Learning Objectives	Speaking Practice	Grammar Note	Page
Lesson.05 **What are you wearing?**	- describe clothing according to seasons - use counting words and adjectives to describe clothing	· I need more….clothes in this weather. · I need a…. · This…is too…for this weather.	Pair terms & Adjectives	32
Lesson.06 **Shopping smart**	- talk about what someone might buy - use active and passive sentences to discuss shopping habits	· This…is a real bargain. · I think it would be cheaper… · Let's look…for a better price.	Active vs. Passive sentences	37
» Review 03				

Unit.04

Lesson Title	Learning Objectives	Speaking Practice	Grammar Note	Page
Lesson.07 **Asking directions**	- ask for directions and discuss routes to different locations - use indirect questions and prepositions of location to ask for directions	· You should try another route. That road is too… · Go straight for…and take…. · What's the…way to get to…?	Indirect questions & Prepositions of location	43
Lesson.08 **Taking public transport**	- purchase tickets and ask for timetables - use wh-questions to request information related to transportation	· Taking…from here is more convenient. · Could you tell me when the next…leaves? · Our city's…system is….	Wh- questions	48
» Review 04				

Unit.05

Lesson Title	Learning Objectives	Speaking Practice	Grammar Note	Page
Lesson.09 **Trending technology**	- compare and discuss new types of technology - use comparatives to describe the differences between different forms of technology	· The new version of the…is…. · Have you upgraded…yet? · It's…than the….	Comparatives	54
Lesson.10 **Can I leave a message?**	- leave and take down a message from a telephone call - use modal verbs to discuss plans and leave messages	· Could I leave a message for…? · Could you have him call me back when…? · Please tell her (him)….	Modal verbs	59
» Review 05				

Unit.06

Lesson Title	Learning Objectives	Speaking Practice	Grammar Note	Page
Lesson.11 **Describing appearance**	- describe the appearances of different people - use adjectives to discuss others' appearance	· She's (He's) the…over there. · She (He) is…and…with…hair. · How would you describe…?	Adjectives	65
Lesson.12 **Describing characteristics**	- describe personality and physical characteristics of people - use adjectives and conjunctions to talk about personalities	· She's (He's) a very…woman (man). · …has a(n)…personality. · I'd describe her (him) as a…woman (man).	Adjectives & Conjunctions	70
» Review 06				

Unit.07

Lesson Title	Learning Objectives	Speaking Practice	Grammar Note	Page
Lesson.13 **I should have…**	- express regrets about the past - use the 3rd conditional to discuss things you wish had gone differently	· …ing…was unfortunate. · I wish I hadn't…. · I shouldn't have….	3rd conditional: "If I had…"	76
Lesson.14 **Special occasions**	- make suggestions for special occasions - use the 2nd conditional to give advice to others	· If I had the money, I would…. · If I had time, I would…. · What would you do if you…?	2nd conditional: "If I were…"	81
» Review 07				

Unit.08

Lesson Title	Learning Objectives	Speaking Practice	Grammar Note	Page
Lesson.15 **Holiday plans**	- make holiday plans - discuss holiday plans using relative clauses	· What are you doing for…? · Are you planning on …for the holidays? · I'm going to…while I'm off work.	Relative clauses	87
Lesson.16 **Getting away**	- discuss the future - tell others about future plans using gerunds	· I'm looking forward to…. · I'm optimistic about…. · I'm ready to start….	Future & Gerunds	92
» Review 08				

Lesson 01

Long time no see!

Learning Objectives:
After studying this lesson, you should be able to...

- ☑ greet old friends and acquaintances

- ☑ use the present continuous to discuss activities you are currently engaged in

1 Getting Started

A | Look at the picture and describe what you can see.

Practice the tongue twister with your partner. Who can say it faster?

» Sally sells sea-shells by the sea-shore. If Sally sells sea-shells by the sea-shore, are you sure the sea-shells that Sally sells are sea-shells for sure?

B | Read the questions below and discuss with your partner.

1. How do you feel when you see a long lost friend?
2. What are some things you might ask or do with a friend you haven't seen for a long time?

2 Vocatree

Look at the words given below, brainstorm the synonyms and antonyms for the words.

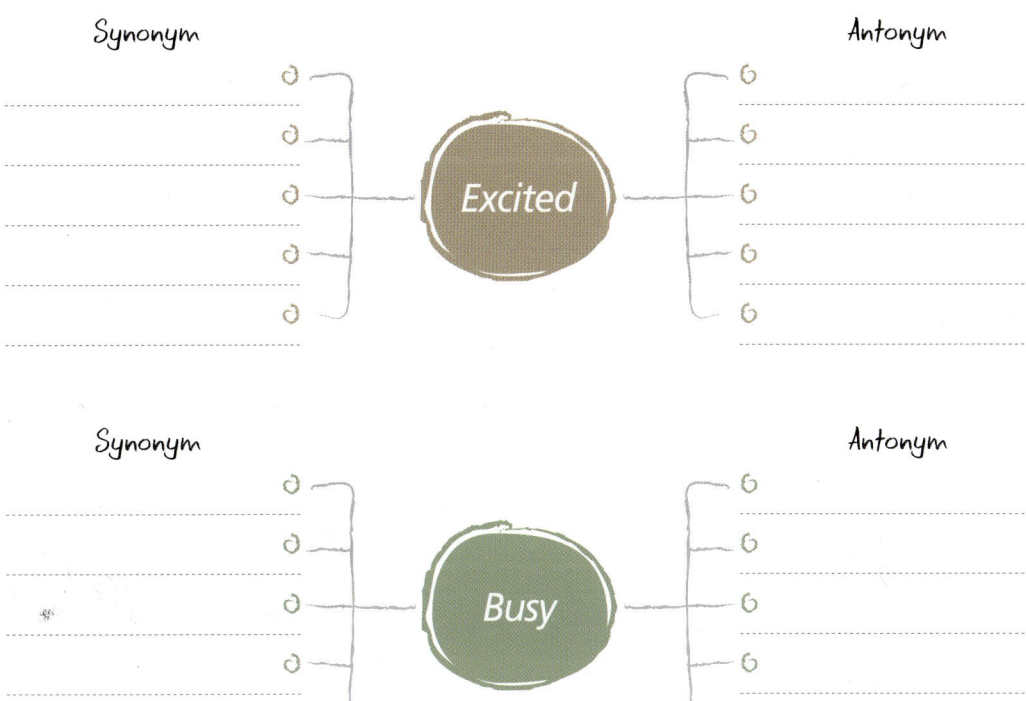

3 Sentence Building

Complete the sentences by filling in the blanks.
Refer to the grammar note note on the right.

1. I'm _____ at a bank now.
2. She _____ taking a Japanese class.
3. _____ you still working at the bookstore?
4. What are _____ doing now?
5. Are you still _____ at the academy?
6. _____ your brother still living at home?
7. I'm _____ at a restaurant three days a week.
8. My sister _____ teaching at a public school.

Grammar Note

Present continuous

» **Are** you **studying** English now?
» I'**m starting** a new job next week.
» How **is** your brother **doing**?
» **Are** you **going** on vacation this summer?

» She'**s attending** graduate school now.
» I'**m taking** a break from work.
» I'**m learning** French now.
» I **am living** with my mother now.

4 Dialogue Practice

Matthew	:	Hey, Jenny! I haven't seen you since graduation!
Jenny	:	I've been busy with graduate school. How is work going?
Matthew	:	I like my new job, but they're transferring me to another office soon.
Jenny	:	Where are you going?
Matthew	:	I'm moving to Europe for a year.
Jenny	:	Europe? Really?
Matthew	:	I know… It's so far away. I was worried that I wouldn't see you before I left.
Jenny	:	Do you have time for coffee? We should catch up.

Comprehension Questions

1. Who is moving?

2. Why haven't the two seen each other for a while? When was the last time they saw each other?

3. What might happen next?

5 Story Board

Look at the situation and complete the conversation.

Situation.01

I haven't seen you since high school! How have things been?

Situation.02

It's been forever! How is your new job going?

6. Comprehensive Listening

Listen to the dialogue and answer the questions.

A Circle True or False

- The two were co-workers.	True False
- Ryan changed jobs.	True False
- Megan and Ryan work in the same office.	True False
- Megan and Ryan will exchange numbers.	True False

B Read the following questions and write full sentence responses.

- When did the two last see each other?

- What does Megan think about her job?

- Where might Megan visit?

- What will John give Megan?

7. Speaking Patterns

Practice using the patterns below with a partner.

I haven't seen you since….
- I haven't seen you since graduation.
- I haven't seen you since December.
- I haven't seen you since I changed jobs.

How is…going?
- How is your business going?
- How is graduate school going?
- How is work going?

I was worried that….
- I was worried that I lost your number.
- I was worried that I wouldn't see you before I moved.
- I was worried that you had forgotten me.

Common Mistakes

What is correct? Read the sentences and circle the correct answer. Check the explanations at the back of the book.

01
I will let you know until tomorrow. / I will let you know by tomorrow.

02
You need to finish dinner by seven. / You need to finish dinner until seven.

03
The children will play soccer until it becomes dark. / The children will play soccer by it becomes dark.

Lesson.01 Long time no see!

8 Situational Use

What are some things you might say in each situation?

Q: What other situations can you think of? Let's think and talk some more!

9 Fun Facts

Greeting Customs Around The World

Did you know?

- The British usually shake hands only when they meet for the first time. A kiss on the cheek is common in informal situations between men and women and also between women who know each other very well.
- The French shake hands with their friends and often kiss them on both cheeks, both upon meeting and leaving.
- In Japan, the common greeting for men and women as well is to bow when they greet someone.
- In Arab countries, close male friends or colleagues hug and kiss both cheeks. They shake hands with the right hand only. Contact between the opposite genders in public is considered obscene.
- Hungarians like to use the friendly greeting form of kissing each other on the cheeks. When men meet for the first time, the casual norm is a firm handshake.
- In Belgium, people kiss on one cheek when they meet, regardless of the gender or how well they know each other.
- In Russia, the typical greeting is a very firm handshake. Assume you're trying to crush each other's knuckles, all the while maintaining direct eye contact.
- In Armenia, by tradition, a woman needs to wait for the man to offer his hand for the handshake. Between good friends and family members, a kiss on the cheek and a light hug are also common.

Question

❶ Which greeting do you find most uncommon or odd? Why?
❷ How would you greet a new acquaintance? What about a close friend?
❸ Describe the do's and don'ts for greetings in your country.

Review and Sneak Peek

Calling
_____
_____

Sneak Peek
01. Have you ever had a pet? Would you like one?
02. What do pets need?

Lesson

02 I'm walking my pet

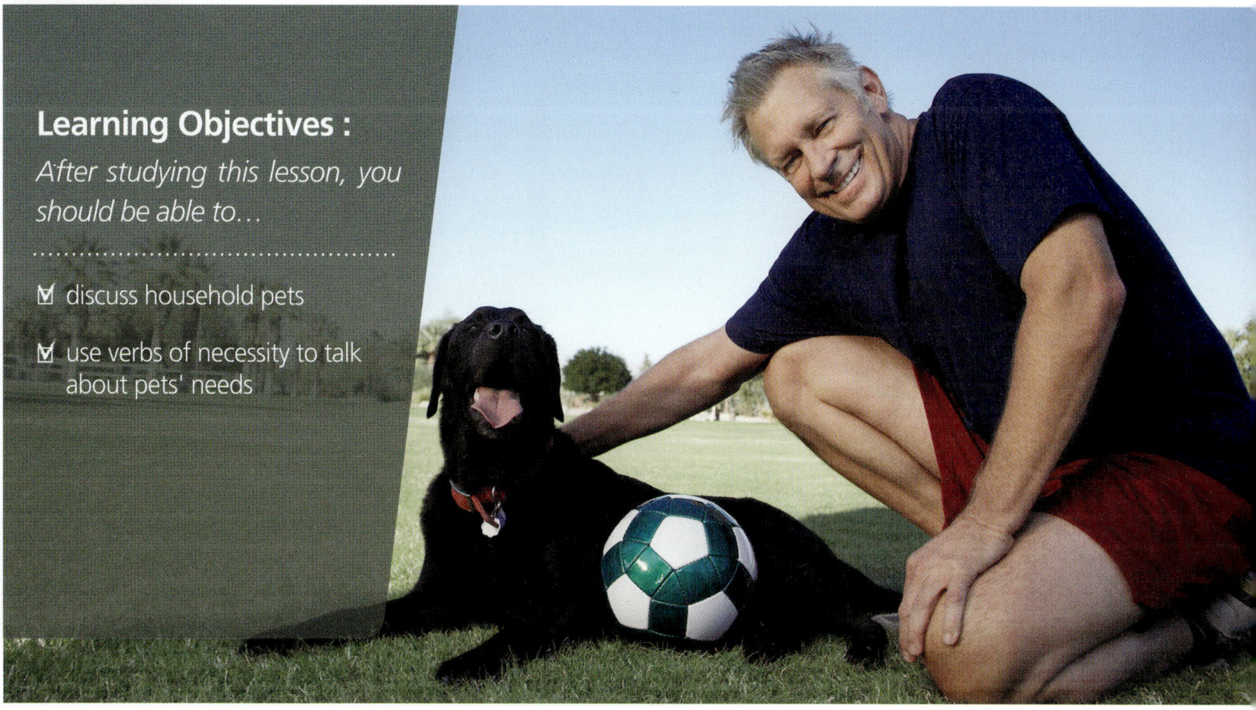

Learning Objectives :

After studying this lesson, you should be able to...

- ☑ discuss household pets
- ☑ use verbs of necessity to talk about pets' needs

1 Getting Started

A | Look at the picture and describe what you can see.

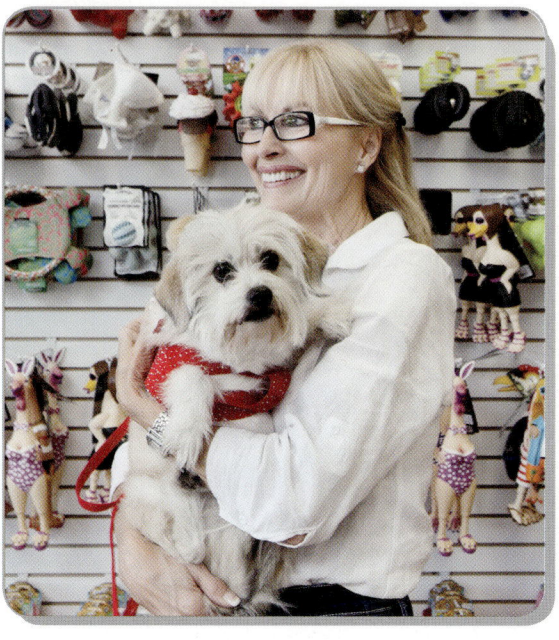

B | Read the questions below and discuss with your partner.

1. Do you have or have you had any pets?
2. What are the advantages or disadvantages of having a pet?

Tongue Twisters

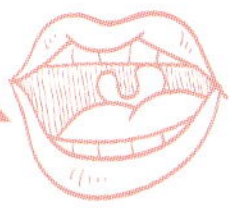

Practice the tongue twister with your partner. Who can say it faster?

» Mr. Tongue Twister tried to train his tongue to twist and turn, to learn the letter "T".

2 Vocatree

Look at the words given below, brainstorm the synonyms and antonyms for the words.

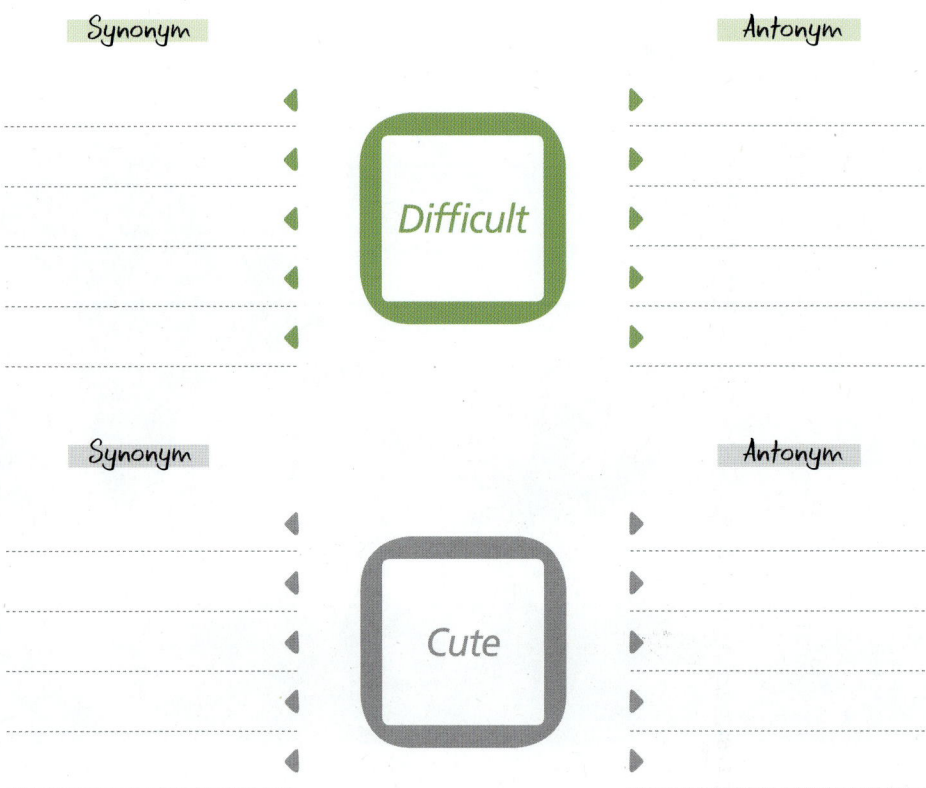

3 Sentence Building

Complete the sentences by filling in the blanks.
Refer to the grammar note note on the right.

1. My father _____ to give water to the pets.

2. I should _____ my dog before I leave the house.

3. We need _____ change the fish's water.

4. My dog _____ some food.

5. We _____ brush the cat's fur.

6. I _____ to change the cat's litter box.

7. I must give my dog some _____ at least once a day.

8. The cats _____ fresh food and water.

Grammar Note

Necessities

» I **have to** feed my dog.
» The birds **need** water.
» We **have to** take our dog to the vet.
» I **should** feed my cat before I go to work.

» I **have to** give my pet some food.
» I **need to** walk my pet twice a day.
» We **should** buy the puppy a new toy.
» My sister **must** change her cat's water every day.

4 Dialogue Practice

Daniel : Are you ready to go to dinner now?

Corey : I need to walk my dog before we go out.

Daniel : How often do you walk your dog?

Corey : I usually walk it twice a day at the park.

Daniel : Your dog is so cute. I bet walking it is fun.

Corey : It is. You should try it some time.

Daniel : I'd like that. Let me know if you ever need help.

Corey : Okay, how about next month? Would you like to walk my dog for me when I visit my mother?

Comprehension Questions

1. What does Corey need to do before dinner?

2. Where might the conversation be taking place?

3. What might happen next?

5 Story Board

Look at the situation and complete the conversation.

Situation.01

Could you wait a minute?

Situation.02

I have a favor to ask you. Could you take care of my dog for me while I'm on vacation?

Lesson.02 I'm walking my pet

6 😊 Comprehensive Listening

Listen to the dialogue and answer the questions.

A Circle True or False

- The man often feeds the dog.   True / False
- They are at the woman's house.   True / False
- They will go to the party together.   True / False
- The woman is ready to leave.   True / False

B Read the following questions and write full sentence responses.

- What does the man do to help?

- Why isn't the woman ready to leave?

- How much food does the dog get?

- Where is the dog food?

7 Speaking Patterns

Practice using the patterns below with a partner.

I…twice a day.
- » I walk it twice a day.
- » I comb its fur twice a day.
- » I feed it twice a day.

I need to…before we go out.
- » I need to walk my dog before we go out.
- » I need to give my cat some water before we go out.
- » I need to feed my hamster before we go out.

Would you…my dog for me?
- » Would you walk my dog for me?
- » Would you feed my dog for me?
- » Would you look after my dog for me?

Common Mistakes

What is correct?
Read the sentences and circle the correct answer.
Check the explanations at the back of the book.

01.
He gave me some help.
/ He gave me any help.

02.
They didn't have some water.
/ They didn't have any water.

03.
Could you give me some help?
/ Could you give me any help?

8 Situational Use

What are some things you might say in each situation?

- With a curious child
- At the pet store
- In the park
- On vacation
- Making small talk
- At the vet

Talking about pets

Q: *What other situations can you think of? Let's think and talk some more!*

9 Fun Facts

Top 5 Peculiar Pets

1 : Madagascar Hissing Cockroach
Some might think this is the grossest pet ever, but many people adore this large, hissing insect. They don't fly or bite, and the hissing sound they make is pretty cool, too. These roaches need small living spaces with places to hide from light and sticks to climb.

2 : Skunk
Skunks have a smelly reputation, but domesticated skunks have their scent glands removed so owners won't have to live with the stench. Skunks are very sensitive and intelligent animals, with curious personalities. Skunks can be litter-trained, just like cats, and eat a mix of fresh veggies and dry food.

3 : Wallaby
The wallaby is an Australian marsupial similar to the kangaroo. They are quite big and can grow up to a meter tall. Wallabies are timid animals that require a lot of open space and diets rich in grass, leaves, and fruits.

4 : Sugar Gliders
Sugar gliders get their name because they can glide from tree to tree. They are very small, weighing only about 85 grams. Sugar gliders love to socialize, so they are happiest in pairs or more. Sugar gliders are nocturnal, so owners may have to stay up at night to bond with their pet.

5 : Potbellied Pig
These pigs are relatively odor-free and easy to train. Potbellies like a routine schedule, so exercise and mealtimes should be at the same times every day. They can be trained to walk on leashes, so these cute pigs can be walked like a dog.

Question

1. Which of the five pets above would you be interested in having? Why?
2. Think of your home and family; what kind of pet would you find suitable?
3. Do you know any other unusual pets? What are they, and what makes them so strange?

Review and Sneak Peek

Calling
_____
_____
_____
_____

Sneak Peek

01.
Where do you do your grocery shopping?

02.
What kind of food do you always keep in your house? Why?

01. Review

- ☐ With your partner, practice greeting a friend you haven't seen in a long time. What do you say?

- ☐ What are some questions you might ask when you met someone for the first time? What about an old friend?

- ☐ What are some customs or manners foreigners should know about greeting people in your country?

- ☐ Use "I was worried that…" "How is…going" patterns to have a conversation with your partner.

- ☐ Do you have a pet? If so, describe it. If not, describe an ideal pet.

- ☐ Do you have a pet? If so, describe it. If not, describe an ideal pet.

- ☐ Describe the advantages or disadvantages of having a pet. Be specific.

- ☐ Use "I…twice a day." "I need to…" patterns to talk about taking care of a pet.

- ☐ What are some strange pets you know of? What makes them unique?

☐ ALL DONE

Lesson 03 — Going grocery shopping

Learning Objectives :
After studying this lesson, you should be able to...

- ☑ learn to ask for prices and describe groceries
- ☑ use intensifiers and superlative adjectives to discuss different products

1 Getting Started

A | Look at the picture and describe what you can see.

B | Read the questions below and discuss with your partner.

1. How often do you go grocery shopping?
2. Where do you usually do your shopping? Why?

Tongue Twisters

Practice the tongue twister with your partner. Who can say it faster?

» Betty bought some butter, but the butter was bitter, so she bought some better butter to make the bitter butter better.

2 Vocatree

Look at the words given below, brainstorm the synonyms and antonyms for the words.

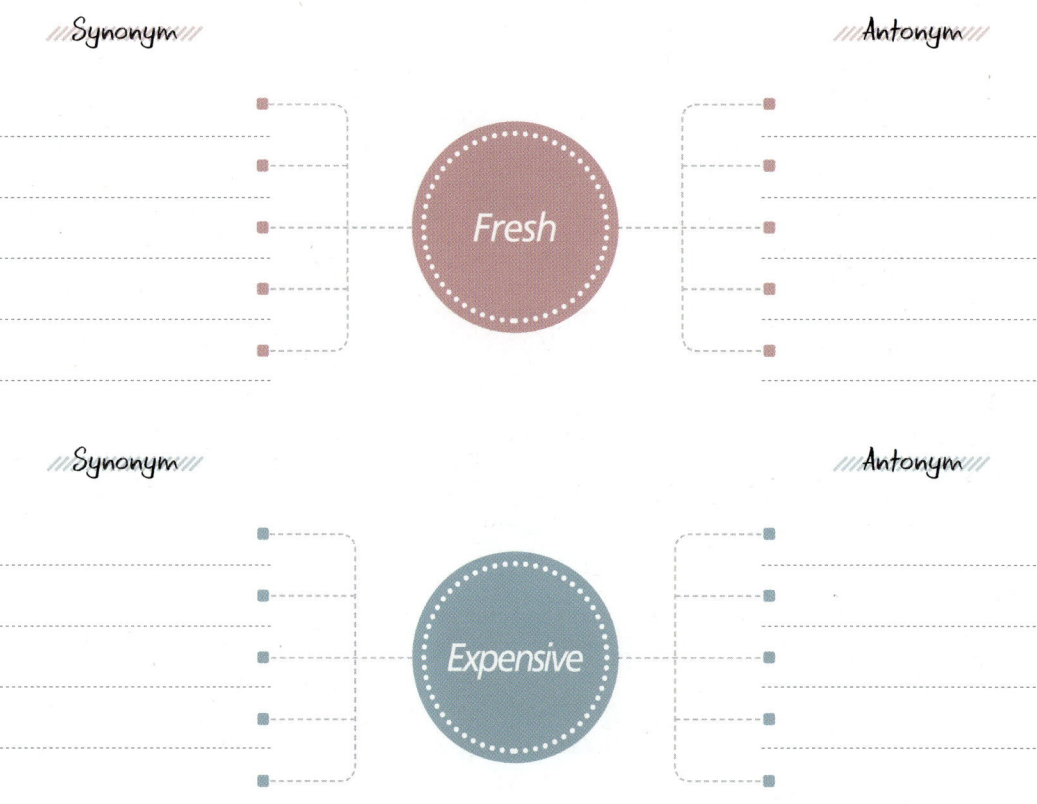

3 Sentence Building

Complete the sentences by filling in the blanks. Refer to the grammar note note on the right.

1. These cucumbers are _____ fresh.

2. This market sells _____ vegetables.

3. I just bought the best pineapple _____ .

4. This is the _____ delicious cake I've ever had.

5. This fruit is extremely _____ .

6. I'm _____ happy I came to this market.

7. These are the _____ berries ever.

8. This meat is _____ good. Could I have some more?

Grammar Note

**Intensifiers
Superlative adjectives**

» *This melon is **extremely** fresh.*
» *This is the **most delicious** bread **ever**.*
» *These cherries are **the sweetest**.*
» *I want to buy some really good **cheese**.*

» *These chips are **very** good.*
» *This is **the best** pizza I've ever tried.*
» *This fish is **incredibly** fresh.*
» *Try these tomatoes. They're **so** great!*

4 Dialogue Practice

Sophia	:	This produce looks very fresh!
Store clerk	:	It's the freshest in town. We get it all from a local farm.
Sophia	:	How much for a kilogram of oranges?
Store clerk	:	They're $4 a kilogram.
Sophia	:	What about the grapefruit?
Store clerk	:	They're also $4.
Sophia	:	Can I mix them? Could you give me half a kilogram of each?
Store clerk	:	Sure thing. Could I bag it for you?

Comprehension Questions

1. What fruit is Sophia interested in?
2. Why might the conversation be taking place?
3. What might Sophia say next?

5 Story Board

Look at the situation and complete the conversation.

Situation.01

Why don't you try this brand? It tastes amazing.

Situation.02

Where do you keep the light bulbs?

Lesson.03 Going grocery shopping

6 Comprehensive Listening

Listen to the dialogue and answer the questions.

A Circle True or False

- The woman is shopping for food.   (*True / False*)
- She will buy two fish.   (*True / False*)
- Her total is $6.   (*True / False*)
- The woman and the man know each other.   (*True / False*)

B Read the following questions and write full sentence responses.

- What does the woman think of the fish?

- Which fish does she want?

- How much does the fish weigh?

- How will the woman pay?

---

7 Speaking Patterns

Practice using the patterns below with a partner.

These (This)…look(s) very fresh.

- » These apples look very fresh.
- » These peaches look very fresh.
- » This fish looks very fresh.

How much for…?

- » How much for a dozen pears?
- » How much for a kilogram of beef?
- » How much for a loaf of bread?

Could you give me…?

- » Could you give me some apples?
- » Could you give me some of that cheese?
- » Could you give me a bottle of water?

Common Mistakes

What is correct? Read the sentences and circle the correct answer. Check the explanations at the back of the book.

01.
Did anyone go to the party?
/ Did any one go to the party?

02.
I can recommend any one of these books. / I can recommend anyone of these books.

03.
Did anyone in the class finish his or her homework?
/ Did any one in the class finish his or her homework?

8 Situational Use

What are some things you might say in each situation?

- With a cashier
- At a farmer's market
- In line at the supermarket
- Talking groceries
- Asking for a discount
- Returning a product
- Planning a party

Q: *What other situations can you think of? Let's think and talk some more!*

9 Fun Facts

7 Must-see Traditional Markets

1. Chatuchak Weekend Market – Bangkok, Thailand
Chatuchak's indoor and outdoor stalls draw 200,000 people each weekend day. From socks to exotic creatures, there's a vast variety of things for sale along the crowded walkways.

2. Grand Bazaar (Kapalı Çarşı) – Istanbul, Turkey
Traders and shoppers have been haggling in this corner of Istanbul for well over 500 years. Narrow, noisy, and packed full of people, this extraordinary market has a manic feel about it.

3. Marché aux Puces de Saint-Ouen – Paris, France
This is one of the world's largest and most interesting collections of antiques and second-hand items. Shoppers are rewarded with affordable one-of-a-kind finds if they just take the time.

4. Chandni Chowk – Delhi, India
Located in the heart of Old Delhi, Chandni Chowk is one of the busiest markets in India. If you can think of an item, any item, it is probably on sale somewhere along this bustling market.

5. Shilin Night Market – Taipei, Taiwan
The largest of Taipei's famous night markets, Shilin Night Market is best known for its gigantic food court. Numerous food stalls serve up local specialities to the never-ending crowds.

6. Flower Market Road – Hong Kong
Flower Market Road is Hong Kong's most picturesque market. The street is lined with thousands of flower varieties – real and fake – from all over the world.

7. Ver-o-Peso – Belém, Brazil
This neo-gothic building beside Belém's docks is home to numerous fishmongers selling the morning's Amazonian catch. Shoppers can also find stalls selling exotic fruits that are hard to come by anywhere else in the world.

Question

1. Which of the markets above would you like to visit? Why?
2. How do you think a traditional market would compare to a shopping mall? What are the advantages and disadvantages?
3. Describe a local market near your neighborhood. What can you buy there? What is the atmosphere like?

Review and Sneak Peek

Calling

_____
_____
_____
_____

Sneak Peek

01.
What does "eating healthily" mean to you? Why?

02.
In your opinion, is eating healthy food important? Explain.

Lesson 04 Healthy eating

Learning Objectives :

After studying this lesson, you should be able to…

☑ talk about healthy eating habits

☑ use adverbs of frequency to discuss healthy eating habits

1 Getting Started

A | Look at the picture and describe what you can see.

Tongue Twisters

Practice the tongue twister with your partner. Who can say it faster?

» How much ground would a groundhog hog, if a groundhog could hog ground? A groundhog would hog all the ground he could hog, if a groundhog could hog ground.

B | Read the questions below and discuss with your partner.

① What kind of food do you like to eat?
② Do you think you have a healthy diet?

2 Vocatree

Look at the words given below, brainstorm the synonyms and antonyms for the words.

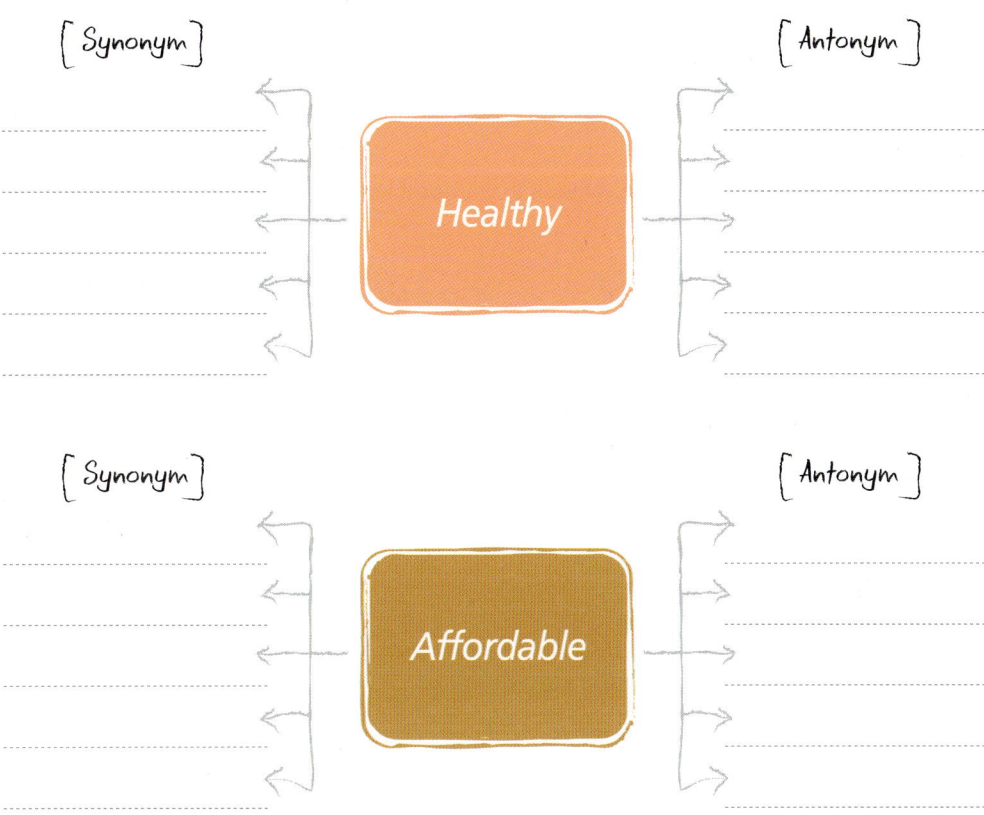

3 Sentence Building

Complete the sentences by filling in the blanks.
Refer to the grammar note note on the right.

1. I eat dessert two or three times a week. I _____ eat dessert.

2. I drink coffee every morning. I _____ drink coffee.

3. My mother dislikes fish, so she _____ eats it.

4. She _____ eats pizza. She eats it a few times a month.

5. My brother drinks cola every day. He _____ drinks it.

6. My sister eats pasta almost every day. She _____ eats it.

7. My family almost never buys sweets. We _____ have them in our house.

Grammar Note

Adverbs of frequency

» I eat salad every two or three days. I **often** eat salad for lunch.

» I eat fresh vegetables almost every day. I **frequently** eat them.

» I almost never eat junk food. I **seldom** eat it.

» I eat breakfast every day. I **always** eat it.

» I drink water many times during the day. I **often** drink it.

» Most of the time, I eat fruit for dessert. I **usually** eat it for dessert.

» I don't eat meat every day. I **sometimes** eat it for dinner.

» I **always** try to eat balanced meals.

4 🎙️ Dialogue Practice

Aiden : I feel so tired lately.

Jacob : You should try eating healthier. Vegetables are good for fatigue.

Aiden : Would that really help?

Jacob : Yes, it would be an affordable solution to your problem.

Aiden : How much should I eat?

Jacob : According to the food pyramid, you should eat at least three servings of vegetables a day.

Aiden : I'm going to try to eat a lot more than that.

Jacob : Don't eat too much. Too much of anything isn't good for you.

Comprehension Questions

1. What is Aiden's problem?

2. What are some reasons that Aiden might be tired?

3. What might Aiden do next?

5 Story Board

Look at the situation and complete the conversation.

Situation.01

You can't have any more ice cream. Too much sugar is not good for you.

Situation.02

How do you stay so healthy? Could you give me any tips?

6 Comprehensive Listening

Listen to the dialogue and answer the questions.

A | Circle True or False

- The man made carrot juice.   True / False
- The man thinks the woman is healthy.   True / False
- There is sugar in the carrot juice.   True / False
- The woman's vision is worth than it was before.   True / False

B | Read the following questions and write full sentence responses.

- What is the woman doing?

....

- Why is the woman's juice healthier than juice sold in stores?

....

- What is the man's problem?

....

- What will the woman do next?

....

7 Speaking Patterns

Practice using the patterns below with a partner.

…is (are) good for…

- » Carrots are good for your eyes.
- » Milk is good for your bones.
- » Spinach is good for your skin.

You should eat…servings of…a day.

- » You should eat three servings of vegetables a day.
- » You should eat two servings of fruit a day.
- » You should eat two servings of dairy a day.

Too much…is not good for you.

- » Too much sugar is not good for you.
- » Too much fat is not good for you.
- » Too much of anything is not good for you.

Common Mistakes

What is correct?
Read the sentences and circle the correct answer.
Check the explanations at the back of the book.

01. ....
I like to see movies.
/ I like to watch movies.

02. ....
I can see the smoke from here.
/ I can watch the smoke from here.

03. ....
I want to watch the stars.
/ I want to see the stars.

8 Situational Use

What are some things you might say in each situation?

Q: What other situations can you think of? Let's think and talk some more!

9 Fun Facts

Understanding the food pyramid

1. Which part of the section of the food pyramid do you enjoy eating? What do you dislike?
2. What are some changes that you can make to your diet for healthier eating?
3. Make a healthy eating plan using the information in the food pyramid.

The food pyramid is designed to make healthy eating easier. Healthy eating is about getting the correct amount of nutrients – protein, fat, carbohydrates, vitamins, and minerals you need to maintain good health.

Healthy eating involves :
- Plenty of bread, rice, potatoes, pasta, and cereals
- Plenty of fruit and vegetables
- Some milk, cheese, and yoghurt
- Some meat, poultry, eggs, beans, and nuts
- A very small amount of fats and oils
- And a very small amount or no food and drinks high in fat, sugar, and salt

Review and Sneak Peek

Calling
_____
_____
_____
_____

Sneak Peek

01.
What is weather like in your country? Explain

02.
How does your summer clothing differ from your winter? Explain.

02. Review

- ☐ How often do you go grocery shopping? What do you usually buy?

- ☐ What kind of fruit do you like? Do you prefer fruit or vegetables?

- ☐ Practice grocery shopping with your partner. Use "How much for…?" "Could you give me…?" patterns.

- ☐ Describe where you do your grocery shopping. Why do you choose to shop there?

- ☐ Do you think you have a healthy diet? Explain.

- ☐ What are some ways you can have a healthier diet? Use "…is (are) good for…" "too much…is not good for you." patterns.

- ☐ Describe your favorite meal. Do you know how to cook it?

- ☐ How often do you eat a home cooked meal? How often do you eat at a restaurant? Which do you prefer?

- ☐ Pretend that you are a nutritionist. Give your partner some healthy eating tips.

☐ ALL DONE

Lesson 05
What are you wearing?

Learning Objectives :

After studying this lesson, you should be able to…

☑ describe clothing according to seasons

☑ use counting words and adjectives to describe clothing

1 Getting Started

A | Look at the picture and describe what you can see.

Practice the tongue twister with your partner. Who can say it faster?

» Whether the weather be fine, or whether the weather be not. Whether the weather be cold, or whether the weather be hot. We'll weather the weather whether we like it or not.

B | Read the questions below and discuss with your partner.

① Describe the clothes you are wearing now. Why did you choose to wear this outfit?

② What do you look at when you are shopping for clothes?

2 Vocatree

Look at the words given below, brainstorm the synonyms and antonyms for the words.

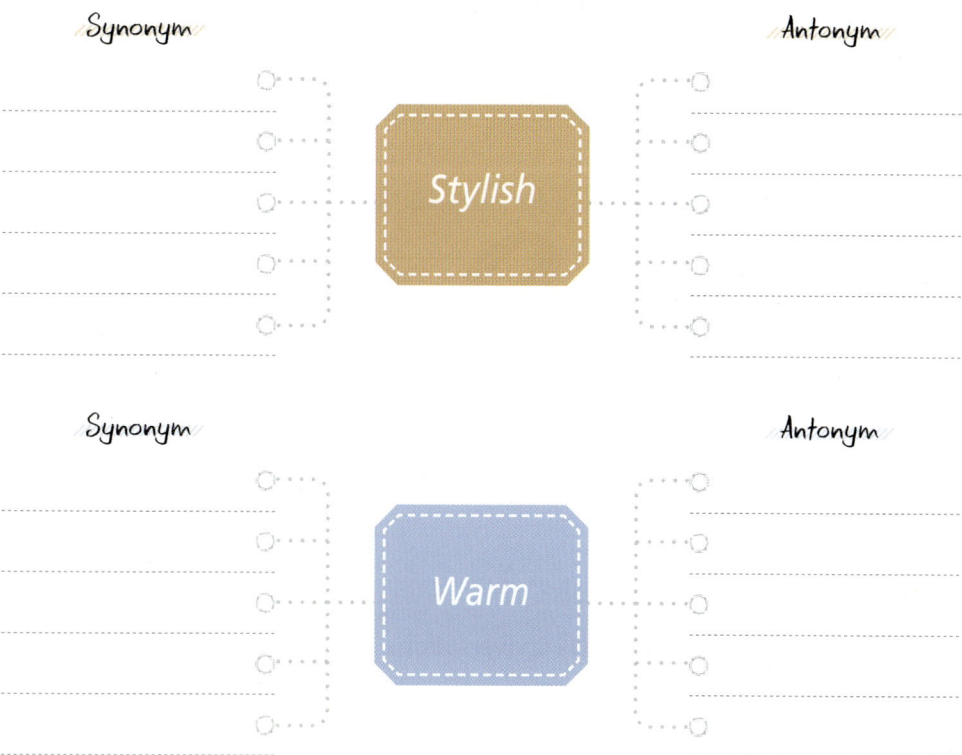

3 Sentence Building

Complete the sentences by filling in the blanks.
Refer to the grammar note note on the right.

1. I bought a new _____ of dress shoes.

2. Our _____ company sweatshirts arrived today.

3. My brother gave me a pair _____ designer sunglasses for my birthday.

4. I love your new pair of running _____ .

5. I want to buy a _____ coat before winter comes.

6. She had on a very tall _____ of boots.

7. I brought an extra pair of _____ in case it rains.

8. That is a very _____ dress.

Grammar Note

Pair terms & Adjectives

» That's a **nice pair of** jeans.
» She has **a lovely** sweater on today.
» I bought **a new pair of** sunglasses for my vacation.
» My company bought all its employees **blue jackets**.

» I gave her **a sparkly** bracelet for her birthday.
» I packed three **pairs of warm** pants for the ski trip.
» Her **stylish jacket** is very **modern**.
» He forgot his **blue pair of** pants at his mother's house.

4 Dialogue Practice

Emily : That's a really nice sweater you have on today.

Logan : Thanks. I bought it yesterday.

Emily : I need more warm clothes in this weather.

Logan : Me, too. It's so cold lately.

Emily : I'm going shopping later. I need a warmer jacket. This one is too light for this weather.

Logan : We should go shopping together.

Emily : I'd like that.

Logan : What time are you going today?

Comprehension Questions

1. When did Logan get his sweater?
2. What season might it be?
3. What might happen after this?

5 Story Board

Look at the situation and complete the conversation.

Situation.01

"I'm so cold now. I really need a heavier coat."

Situation.02

"What do you think of this dress."

| 34 | Pre Get Up To Speed 2

6 Comprehensive Listening

Listen to the dialogue and answer the questions.

A Circle True or False

- The man and woman went shopping together.   True / False
- He will buy warmer clothes for summer.   True / False
- The weather is very hot.   True / False
- The woman helps the man find his size.   True / False

B Read the following questions and write full sentence responses.

- Where does the conversation take place?

- What will the man try on?

- What is the man shopping for?

- What does the woman think of the first shirt?

7 Speaking Patterns

Practice using the patterns below with a partner.

I need more…clothes in this weather.
- I need more warm clothes in this weather.
- I need more cool clothes in this weather.
- I need more winter clothes in this weather.

I need a….
- I need a warmer jacket.
- I need a new bathing suit.
- I need a pair of shorts.

This…is too…for this weather.
- This coat is too warm for this weather.
- This jacket is too light for this weather.
- This suit is too heavy for this weather.

Common Mistakes

What is correct?
Read the sentences and circle the correct answer.
Check the explanations at the back of the book.

01
When you leave, make sure you take an umbrella. / When you leave, make sure you bring an umbrella.

02
Can you take some souvenirs for us? / Can you bring some souvenirs for us?

03
When you go to the dinner party, take a bottle of wine. / When you go to the dinner party, bring a bottle of wine.

8 Situational Use

What are some things you might say in each situation?

Q: What other situations can you think of? Let's think and talk some more!

9 Fun Facts

Here are some trending Fashion statistics

- The world clothing and textile industry (clothing, textiles, footwear and luxury goods) reached almost $2,560 trillion in 2010.
- In 2010, American households spent, on average, $1,700 on apparel, footwear, and related products and services.
- Catherine, Duchess of Cambridge, spent more than $54,000 on clothes in less than 6 months.
- Consumers in the United Kingdom have an estimated $46.7 billion worth of unworn clothes lingering in their closets.
- The Chinese textile industry creates about 3 billion tons of soot each year.
- Millions of tons of unused fabric at Chinese mills go to waste each year when dyed the wrong color.
- Over 232,000 people attend New York Fashion Week per year and over $20 million is funneled into the New York City economy during fashion week.
- Germany had the highest hourly pay for those working in the clothing manufacturing industry and the Philippines, with payment at 88 cents per hour, had the lowest.

 Question

1. Which statistic is surprising to you? What is expected?
2. How much do you think you spend on clothing and accessories each year? How does this compare to your partner?
3. What do you prefer to wear? Describe your fashion style or preference.

Review and Sneak Peek

Calling

_____
_____
_____
_____

Sneak Peek

01.
How often do you go shopping?

02.
What are your favorite products to buy? Explain.

Lesson 06 Shopping smart

Learning Objectives :

After studying this lesson, you should be able to…

- ☑ talk about what someone might buy
- ☑ use active and passive sentences to discuss shopping habits

1 Getting Started

A | Look at the picture and describe what you can see.

B | Read the questions below and discuss with your partner.

① Do you enjoy shopping? How often do you go shopping?

② Where do you usually go shopping? With whom do you go?

Practice the tongue twister with your partner. Who can say it faster?

» Mr. See owned a saw, and Mr. Soar owned a seesaw. Now, See's saw sawed Soar's seesaw before Soar saw See.

2 Vocatree

Look at the words given below, brainstorm the synonyms and antonyms for the words.

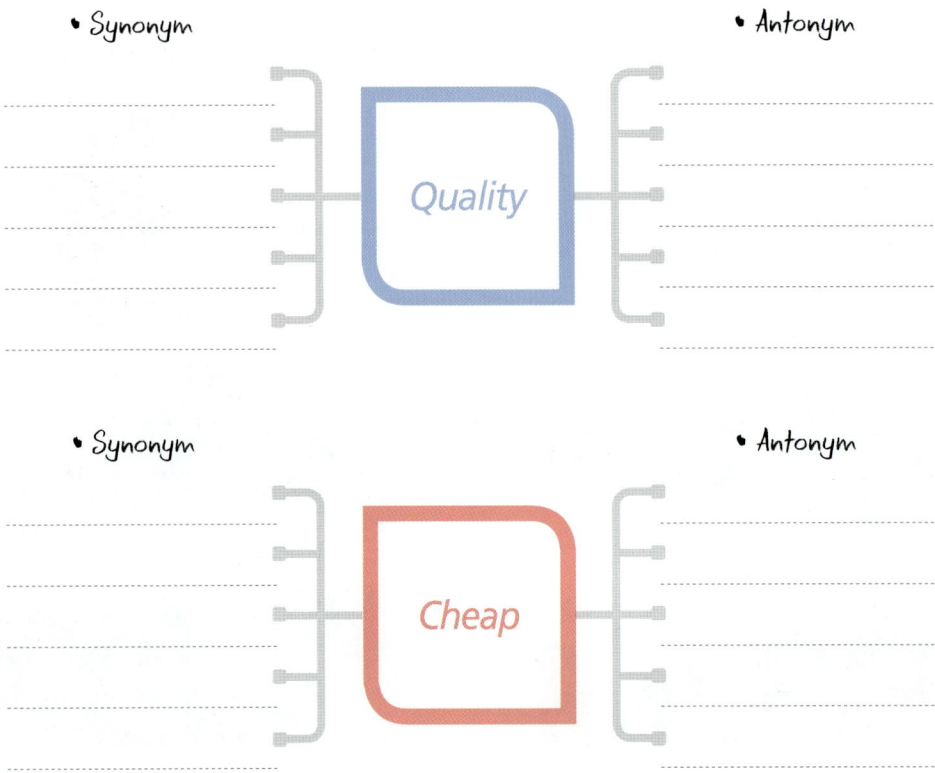

3 Sentence Building

Complete the sentences by filling in the blanks.
Refer to the grammar note note on the right.

1. The furniture was _____ for me by my brother.
2. I _____ the outlet last month.
3. She _____ her new bag from a website.
4. I _____ my friend about the new outlet mall.
5. That new car _____ purchased by my boss.
6. My new phone was _____ with a credit card.
7. My brother _____ a new car for his birthday.
8. My sister's phone is paid for _____ my parents.

Grammar Note

Active vs. Passive sentences

» I **purchased** some new boots last week.
» I often **go** shopping on the weekend.
» That phone was purchas**ed by** me.
» He **got** some milk at the market.

» I **told** her about the new store's grand opening.
» That new car **was** bought **by** my mother.
» I often **order** my clothes on the internet.
» I **was** told about the sale **by** my friend.

4 Dialogue Practice

Mia : This coat is a real bargain, don't you think?

Charlotte : I'm not sure…. It will probably get cheaper. Winter is almost over.

Mia : I guess so.

Charlotte : Let's look around some more for a better price.

Mia : Where could I look?

Charlotte : I think it would be cheaper online.

Mia : Maybe… I really like it though.

Charlotte : You can always buy it later if you can't find it cheaper.

Comprehension Questions

1. What does Mia want?
2. Do you think Charlotte really likes the coat? Why or why not?
3. What might happen next?

5 Story Board

Look at the situation and complete the conversation.

Situation.01

How about this TV? Is it a good price?

Situation.02

This sale is great!

6 Comprehensive Listening

Listen to the dialogue and answer the questions.

A. Circle True or False

- The man and woman are shopping for a new TV.   (True / False)
- The woman doesn't think they need a new TV.   (True / False)
- The store's TV is bigger than their current one. (True / False)
- The woman thinks a bigger TV would be nice.   (True / False)

B. Read the following questions and write full sentence responses.

- What is the couple talking about?

- Where does the woman think the TV would be cheaper?

- Why doesn't the woman think they need a new TV now?

- What does the man think of the TV?

7 Speaking Patterns

Practice using the patterns below with a partner.

This…is a real bargain.
- This steak is a real bargain.
- This coat is a real bargain.
- This handbag is a real bargain.

I think it would be cheaper…
- I think it would be cheaper online.
- I think it would be cheaper at a bigger supermarket.
- I think it would be cheaper at the market.

Let's look…for a better price.
- Let's look on the Internet for a better price.
- Let's look around for a better price.
- Let's look some more for a better price.

Common Mistakes

What is correct?
Read the sentences and circle the correct answer.
Check the explanations at the back of the book.

01 The camel was lost in the desert. / The camel was lost in the dessert.

02 Desert is my favorite part of the meal. / Dessert is my favorite part of the meal.

03 There is very little rainfall in the desert. / There is very little rainfall in the dessert.

8 Situational Use

What are some things you might say in each situation?

- Discussing new products
- Talking about sales
- Complimenting others
- With friends at lunch
- Making weekend plans
- Discussing purchases

Talking about shopping

Q: *What other situations can you think of? Let's think and talk some more!*

9 Fun Facts

Smart Shopping Tips

Everyone wants to save money when they shop. The best way to save money is to plan ahead. Here are some tips you can use to save money!

01
Shop with a list. Before you set off on your shopping trip, look what you already have, then write a list of the things you MUST buy.

02
Set a budget. Many people overspend on things they don't want, need, or use because they have no specific limit to their spending. Set a budget and stop shopping once you hit that limit.

03
Set a timeframe. Don't allow yourself to wander around aimlessly. Set a specific time for your shopping, and once that time is over, finish your shopping. Remember, time is gold!

04
Don't shop when you are tired, hungry, lonely, bored, or upset. These are some of the common emotional triggers that cause people to shop unconsciously and unwisely.

05
Don't buy just because it's on sale. "Sale" really is a four-letter word! Remember that a bargain is not a bargain if it's not really needed. Only buy items on sale when it's something that is on your list and is within your budget.

Question
1. Do you usually plan ahead before going shopping? If so, what do you prepare?
2. Which of the tips do you agree or disagree with? Explain.
3. Add another tip to the list. Give an explanation why.

Review and Sneak Peek

Calling
_____
_____
_____
_____

Sneak Peek
01.
When do you need to give directions? Explain.

02.
How do you go home from here? Describe it in detail.

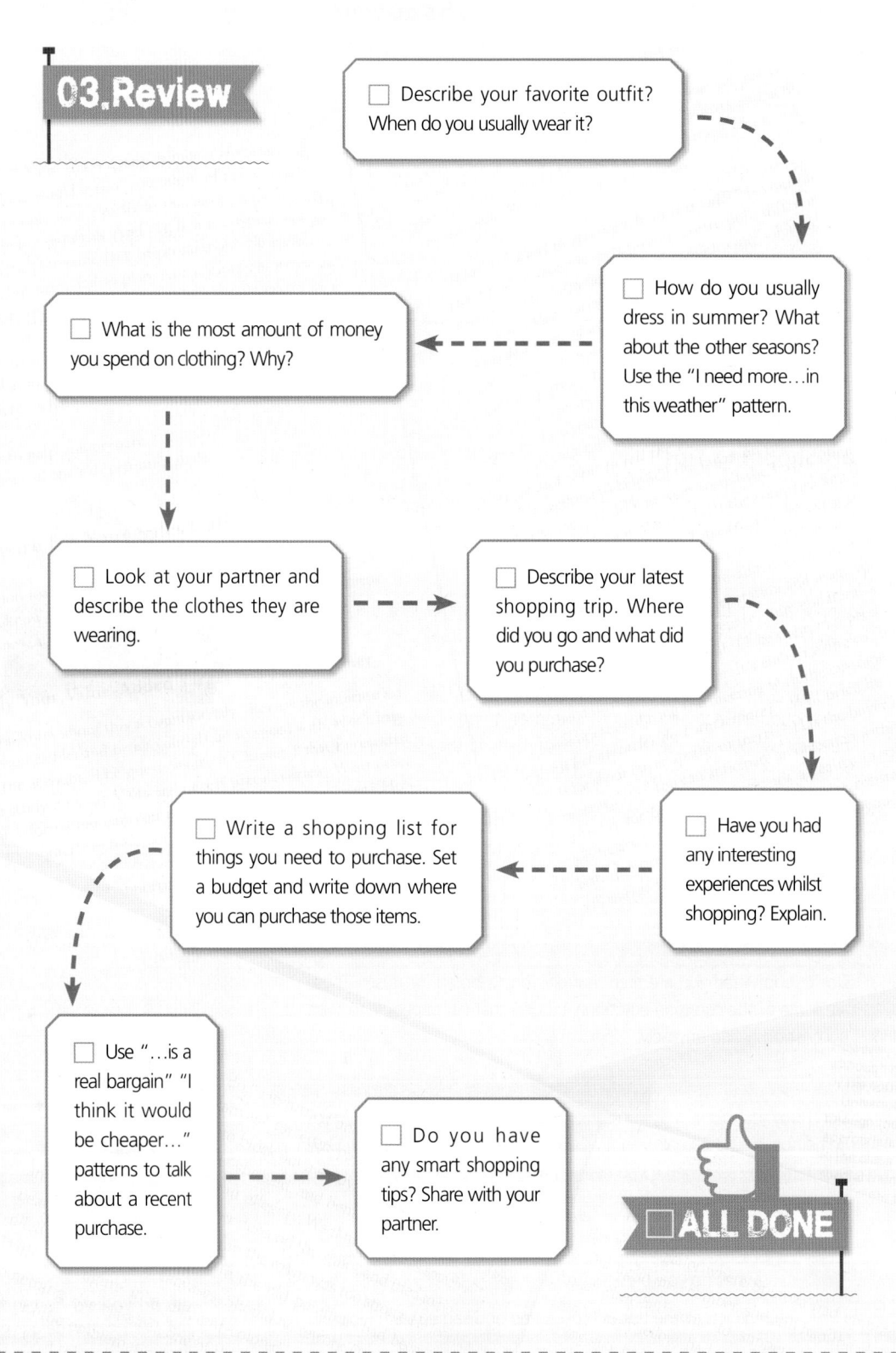

Lesson 07 — Asking directions

Learning Objectives :
After studying this lesson, you should be able to...

- ask for directions and discuss routes to different locations
- use indirect questions and prepositions of location to ask for directions

1 Getting Started

A | **Look at the picture and describe what you can see.**

B | **Read the questions below and discuss with your partner.**

1. Are you good with directions? What do you do if you get lost?
2. Describe a situation when you were lost. What happened?

Practice the tongue twister with your partner. Who can say it faster?

» If Pickford's packers packed a packet of chips would the packet of chips that Pickford's packers packed survive for two and a half years?

2 Vocatree

Look at the words given below, brainstorm the synonyms and antonyms for the words.

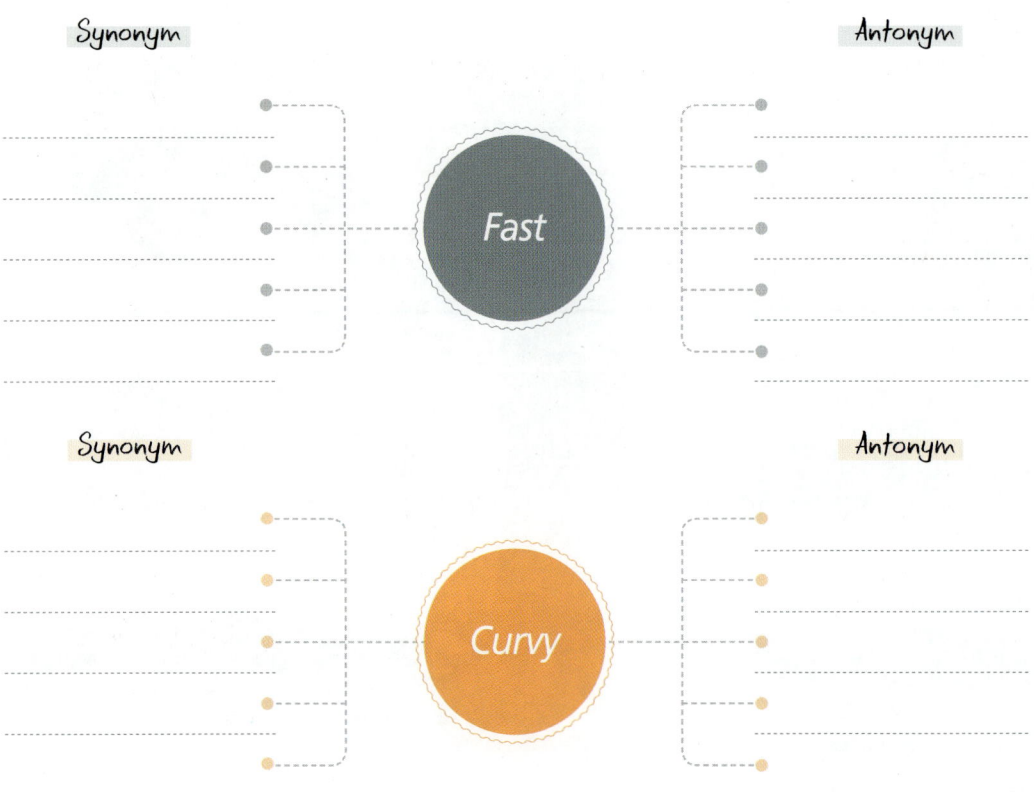

3 Sentence Building

Complete the sentences by filling in the blanks. Refer to the grammar note note on the right.

1. If you have _____, let me know where to meet you.

2. Could you _____ me know a faster way to get to the bank?

3. I _____ her to drive straight for 5 minutes and turn right.

4. Do you _____ where the post office is?

5. I'd _____ it if you could give me directions.

6. _____ you tell me the address again?

7. Go straight for three blocks and turn left. The gas station is _____ to the grocery store.

8. The man told me to go around the _____.

Grammar Note

Indirect questions & Prepositions of location

» **Could you tell me** where the store is?
» He told me it's **next to** the bank.
» **I wondered if you could tell me** a faster route.
» I told her to go **down** the street.
» The GPS told me to go **straight** for three blocks.
» **If you can**, e-mail me directions to the hotel.
» **I'd like it if you** told me where I should park.
» She told me to go **around** the corner.
» **Do you know** what street it is on?

4. Dialogue Practice

Lily : I just realized what time it is…. I'm going to be late to my meeting.

Oliver : Where are you going? I might know a shortcut.

Lily : What's the best way to get to the Butler Building from here?

Oliver : Go straight for three blocks on Riverside Drive and take a right.

Baylor : I think you should try another route. That road is too curvy to drive quickly on.

Lily : What do you recommend?

Baylor : How about down Martin Street?

Oliver : I agree. That might be better…

Lily : I'll try that. Thanks so much!

Comprehension Questions

1. Where is Lily going?
2. What time of day might this conversation be taking place?
3. What might happen next?

5. Story Board

Look at the situation and complete the conversation.

Situation.01

It's almost rush hour. Should I take the expressway?

Situation.02

You look lost. Where are you trying to go?

Lesson.07 Asking directions

6 Comprehensive Listening

Listen to the dialogue and answer the questions.

A Circle True or False

- The man wants to take the old highway first.	True / False
- The woman recommends a new route.	True / False
- The expressway is faster.	True / False
- The man will fly in an airplane.	True / False

B Read each question and write full sentence responses.

- What is the conversation about?

- What is the man's problem?

- What is wrong with the expressway?

- Why is the old highway better?

7 Speaking Patterns

Practice using the patterns below with a partner.

You should try another route. That road is too…

- » You should try another route. That road is too curvy.
- » You should try another route. That road is too dangerous.
- » You should try another route. That road is too crowded.

Go straight for…and take….

- » Go straight for ten minutes and take a right.
- » Go straight for three kilometers and take a left.
- » Go straight for five blocks and take the stairs on your right.

What's the…way to get to…?

- » What's the fastest way to get to the supermarket?
- » What's the shortest way to get to the expressway?
- » What's the best way to get to the office?

Common Mistakes

What is correct?
Read the sentences and circle the correct answer.
Check the explanations at the back of the book.

01.
Let's go shopping at the mall. / Lets go shopping at the mall.

02.
He let's his students run in the classroom. / He lets his students run in the classroom.

03.
The boy let's the dog sleep on the bed. / The boy lets the dog sleep on the bed.

8 Situational Use

What are some things you might say in each situation?

- Being lost in a foreign city
- Looking for a restaurant
- Visiting a friend's home

Asking directions

- On vacation
- Making a plan
- While running late

Q: What other situations can you think of? Let's think and talk some more!

9 Fun Facts

Lose Yourself in the World's Most Captivating Mazes

01. Hampton Court, England
Commissioned around 1700, it's the oldest surviving maze in the United Kingdom. In 2005, audio installation was added to heighten the experience of getting lost.

02. Davis Mega Mystery Maze, United States
A zip-line, rope course, and double-decker bridge as well as the usual twists and turns are some of the distinguishable features of this maze.

03. Il Labirinto Stra, Italy
The hedges of this maze, which form nine concentric rings, are too high for anyone to peek over. A perfect view can be enjoyed from the top of the 18th century turret at the center of the maze.

04. The Tangled Maze, Australia
Unlike other basic hedge mazes, this one comes with seasonal variations—ornamental grapes in autumn ring the changes with clematis and wisteria in the Australian spring.

05. Green Man Maze, Wales
This maze is attached to Penpont, a mansion that has been in the same family since 1966, and was commissioned from a local artist to celebrate the Millennium.

Review and Sneak Peek

Calling
_____
_____
_____
_____

Sneak Peek

01.
What is your favorite form of transportation? Explain.

02.
How often do you travel? Where do you want to go next?

Question

❶ How do you feel about mazes? Do you like them or dislike them?

❷ Choose a maze from the list that you would like to visit. What is the reason for your choice?

❸ Imagine you are lost in a maze. You are only allowed to try three things to escape from it. What would you do?

Lesson 08
Taking public transport

Learning Objectives :
After studying this lesson, you should be able to…

☑ purchase tickets and ask for timetables

☑ use wh-questions to request information related to transportation

1 Getting Started

A | **Look at the picture and describe what you can see.**

 Tongue Twisters

Practice the tongue twister with your partner. Who can say it faster?

» How many cans can a kangaroo nibble, if a kangaroo can nibble cans? As many cans as a kangaroo can nibble if a kangaroo can nibble cans.

B | **Read the questions below and discuss with your partner.**

① What means of transport do you usually use? Why?

② List the various public transport services your city provides. Describe their features.

2 Vocatree

Look at the words given below, brainstorm the synonyms and antonyms for the words.

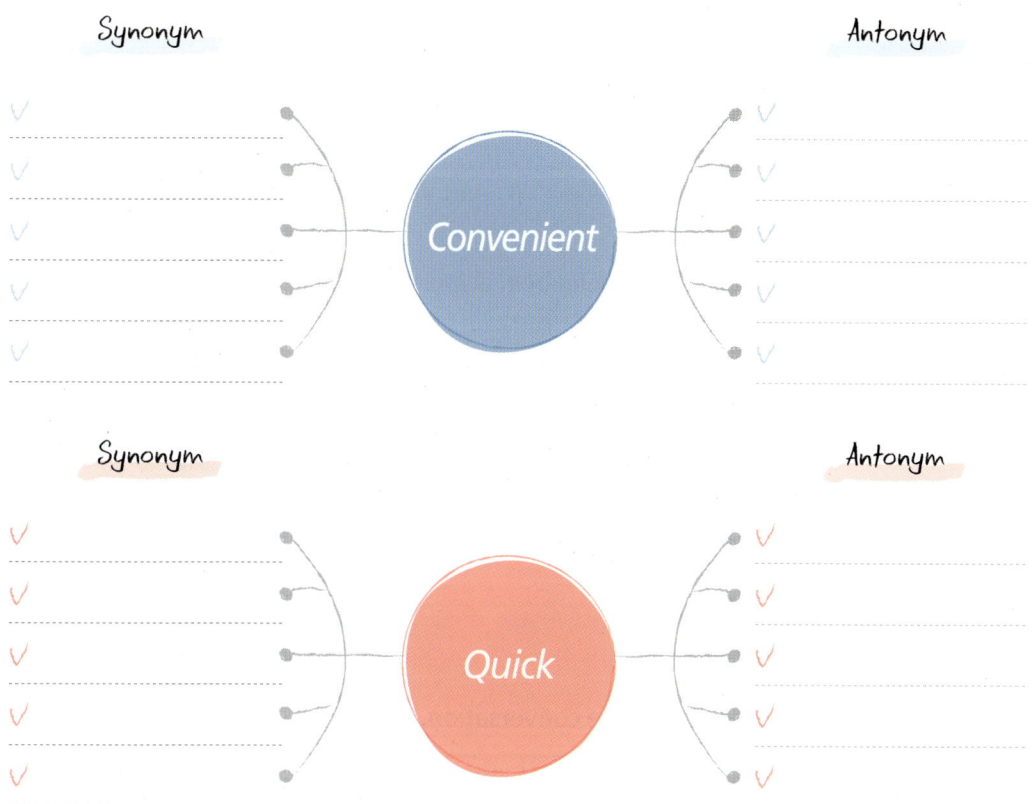

3 Sentence Building

Complete the sentences by filling in the blanks. Refer to the grammar note note on the right.

1. How much _____ does the bus take?

2. When _____ we leave for our train?

3. Where can I _____ the train?

4. What is the _____ bus stop?

5. _____ does our flight leave?

6. When should we _____ to go home?

7. _____ can I find an ATM?

8. How can I _____ to the airport?

Grammar Note

Wh - questions

» **How much time does** it take to get to the expressway from here?
» **When** does the bus arrive?
» **Where** is the nearest post office?
» **What** is the nearest bank?
» **Where can** I take a bus near here?

» **When should** I leave if I need to get to the airport by 4:00?
» **Where** can I find a supermarket?
» **What time does** the next train for Hartford leave?
» **How can I get to** the grocery store?

4 Dialogue Practice

Hotel Concierge	:	How may I help you?
Braden	:	Could you help me get a taxi to the airport?
Hotel Concierge	:	There's a lot of traffic now, so I think taking the bus from here is more convenient.
Braden	:	Really? Could you tell me when the next bus leaves?
Hotel Concierge	:	It leaves every 30 minutes from in front of the hotel. The next one is at 1 p.m.
Braden	:	Is it expensive?
Hotel Concierge	:	No, it's only $3. Our city's public transportation system is affordable.
Braden	:	Can I buy tickets on the bus?

Comprehension Questions

1. How does Braden want to go to the airport?
2. Why might he want to take a taxi?
3. What might happen next?

5 Story Board

Look at the situation and complete the conversation.

Situation.01

How may I help you?

BUS TICKET

Situation.02

The bus is late again!

BUS STOP

6 Comprehensive Listening

Listen to the dialogue and answer the questions.

A | Circle True or False

- The bus costs $1. True / False
- The man will take the bus. True / False
- The bus is closer than the subway. True / False
- The woman prefers the subway. True / False

B | Read the following questions and write full sentence responses.

- What is the woman looking for?

- Why does the man say to take the bus?

- When does the next bus leave?

- What does the man think of the city's buses?

7 Speaking Patterns

Practice using the patterns below with a partner.

Taking…from here is more convenient.
- Taking a taxi from here is more convenient.
- Taking a bus from here is more convenient.
- Taking the subway from here is more convenient.

Could you tell me when the next…leaves?
- Could you tell me when the next bus leaves?
- Could you tell me when the next shuttle leaves?
- Could you tell me when the next train leaves?

Our city's…system is….
- Our city's public transportation system is affordable.
- Our city's subway system is complex.
- Our city's bus system is inconvenient.

Common Mistakes

What is correct?
Read the sentences and circle the correct answer.
Check the explanations at the back of the book.

---------- 01
I wonder how the weather is in France. / I wonder how the whether is in France.

---------- 02
Weather the boy ate the chocolate remained a mystery. / Whether the boy ate the chocolate remained a mystery.

---------- 03
I'm not sure weather you will like it or not. / I'm not sure whether you will like it or not.

8 Situational Use

What are some things you might say in each situation?

Q: What other situations can you think of? Let's think and talk some more!

9 Fun Facts

Annual Subway Ridership

Did you know?

01. In Japan, there are metro cars reserved only for women. (Other countries including Egypt, India, Iran, Taiwan, Brazil, Mexico, Indonesia, Malaysia, and United Arab Emirates have also implemented women-only sections of transportation.)

02. It is illegal to eat, drink, or smoke on the Washington D.C. metro because of the extra costs associated with cleaning the carpet.

03. The Moscow metro is known to have the most beautiful stations in the world.

04. The London Underground is the world's oldest metro system.

05. The New York City subway, with 468 stations, is the largest subway system by number of stations.

06. The Seoul metro is the world's largest in terms of passenger-route length.

07. The Arsenalna metro station in Kiev, Ukraine, is the world's deepest metro station, at 346 feet (105.5 meters) underground.

08. The Copenhagen metro is a 24/7 driverless electric system with a sweet view.

09. The word "metro" actually comes from an abbreviated form of the "Paris Metropolitan."

10. There are currently four cities on the African continent with metro lines.

01. Tokyo	3.334 billion
02. Beijing	3.209 billion
03. Seoul	2.560 billion
04. Shanghai	2.500 billion
05. Moscow	2.491 billion
06. Guangzhou	1.990 billion
07. New York City	1.708 billion
08. Mexico City	1.685 billion
09. Hong Kong	1.600 billion
10. Paris	1.541 billion

Question

❶ Which information above is most striking to you?

❷ What is a problem that you have faced while using the metro system? What are some solutions?

❸ The information above is about the metro system. Choose and discuss the advantages and disadvantages of other transportation methods.

Review and Sneak Peek

Calling
_____
_____
_____
_____

Sneak Peek

01.
What types of technology are you interested in? Why?

02.
What features do you look for when you buy a new phone? Explain.

04. Review

- [ ] How would you rate your ability to read maps and follow directions? Explain.

- [ ] Men are better than women at following directions. Do you agree or disagree? Explain why

- [ ] Give directions to your work place or home. Use "What's the…way to get to…?" "Go straight for…take…" patterns.

- [ ] Describe an experience where you were lost. What did you do?

- [ ] How often do you use public transport? What do you use?

- [ ] Introduce the public transport services that your city or home town has. Be sure to use "Our city's…system is…" "Taking…from here is more convenient." Patterns.

- [ ] Describe your daily commute to work or school. What advice would you give someone who is taking the same route as you?

- [ ] What are some ideas you could give your city council to make traveling with public transport more convenient?

- [ ] What do you think are the advantages and disadvantages of using public transport? Explain.

- [ ] ALL DONE

Lesson 09

Trending technology

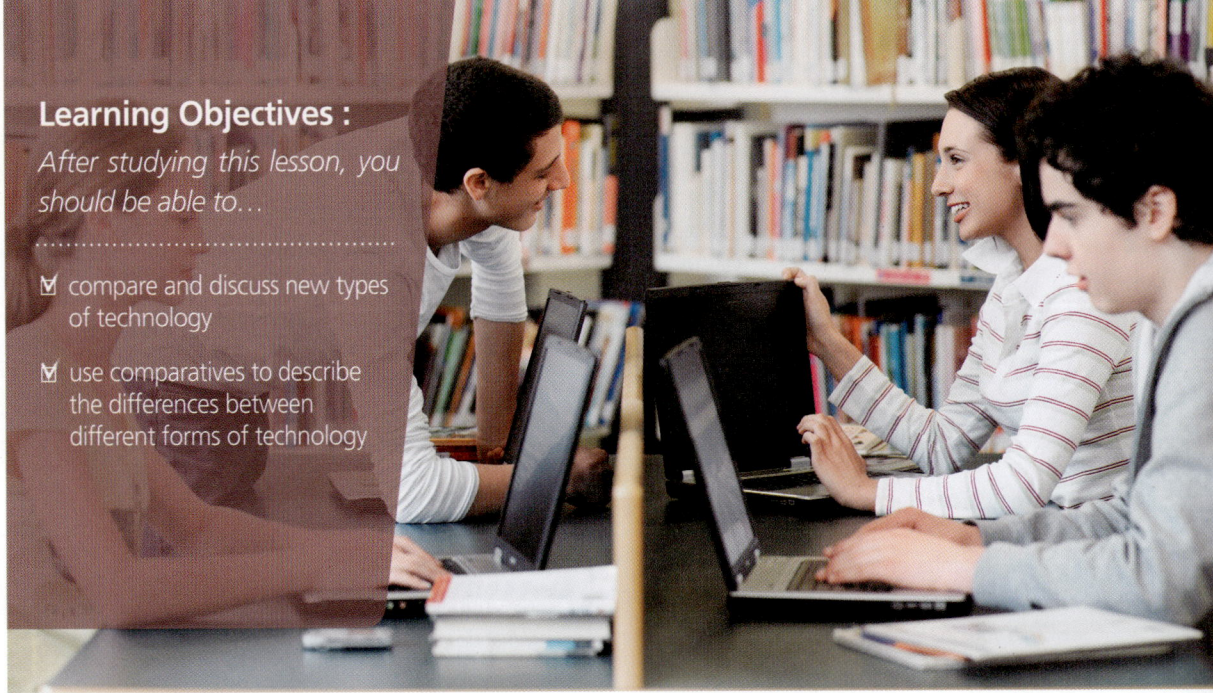

Learning Objectives:
After studying this lesson, you should be able to...

☑ compare and discuss new types of technology

☑ use comparatives to describe the differences between different forms of technology

1 Getting Started

A | Look at the picture and describe what you can see.

Practice the tongue twister with your partner. Who can say it faster?

» There was a fisherman named Fisher who fished for some fish in a fissure. Until a fish with a grin, pulled the fisherman in. Now they're fishing the fissure for Fisher.

B | Read the questions below and discuss with your partner.

① Do you think you are tech savvy? What are some new products that you use?

② How do you feel about new technology? What are the advantages or disadvantages of new technologies?

2 Vocatree

Look at the words given below, brainstorm the synonyms and antonyms for the words.

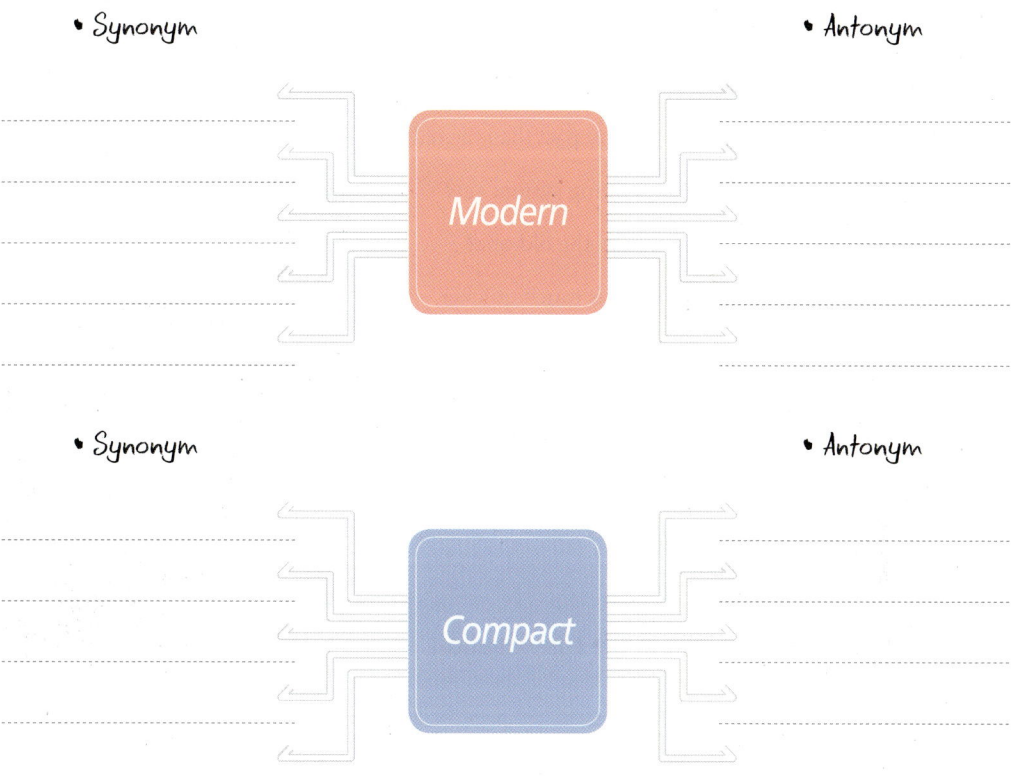

3 Sentence Building

Complete the sentences by filling in the blanks.
Refer to the grammar note note on the right.

1. I bought this phone because it is faster _____ other models.

2. The software is much _____ advanced than previous versions.

3. My brother's phone is much _____ than mine.

4. The quality of this computer is much _____ than the other one.

5. My computer is so heavy. I want to buy a _____ one.

6. The new program is much _____ than the old one.

7. I like this model _____ than that one.

8. Our office's old computers cost a lot of money. They were more _____ than our new ones.

Grammar Note

Comparatives

» My new phone is **lighter than** my old.
» My father likes his old phone **more than** his new one.
» This model is **faster than** the last.
» I think this new program is **better**.
» She recommended this computer because it is **more advanced**.

» My work computer is much **slower** than my personal one.
» This design is **more intelligent** than other models.
» I think the quality of these headphones is **higher**.
» The notebook looks **simpler** than the last, but it is much **better**.

4. Dialogue Practice

Hannah : Did you change phones?
Gavin : Yes, I got a new one last month.
Hannah : Ah … you have the same one as me.
Gavin : I really like it. It's much more compact than the old one.
Hannah : Have you upgraded the operating system yet?
Gavin : No … is it much different than the old one?
Hannah : Not very, but the new version is much quicker.
Gavin : Could you help me update it?

Comprehension Questions

1. What are they talking about?
2. Why might Gavin like his new phone?
3. What might Hannah say next?

5. Story Board

Look at the situation and complete the conversation.

Situation.01

How do you like your new phone?

Situation.02

This program is so slow!

6 Comprehensive Listening

Listen to the dialogue and answer the questions.

A Circle True or False

- The woman wants a new phone.   True / False
- The man's phone is old.   True / False
- He bought new software for his phone.   True / False
- He is happy with the phone's price.   True / False

B Read the following questions and write full sentence responses.

- What is the conversation about?

....

- When did the man buy the phone?

....

- What does the man think about the phone's cost?

....

- What might the woman want to do?

....

7 Speaking Patterns

Practice using the patterns below with a partner.

The new version of the…is….

- » The new version of the program is much quicker.
- » The new version of the phone is much lighter.
- » The new version of the software is easier to use.

Have you upgraded…yet?

- » Have you upgraded your phone yet?
- » Have you upgraded the software yet?
- » Have you upgraded the program yet?

It's…than the….

- » It's more compact than the old one.
- » It's much cheaper than the other model.
- » It's easier to use than the other brand.

Common Mistakes

What is correct?
Read the sentences and circle the correct answer.
Check the explanations at the back of the book.

01
I think lightening the color of your hair is a good idea. / I think lightning the color of your hair is a good idea.

02
The boy was afraid of the lightening. / The boy was afraid of the lightning.

03
Her face lightened after hearing the news. / Her face lightned after hearing the news.

8 Situational Use

What are some things you might say in each situation?

- At an electronics store
- Giving advice to an older relative
- Complimenting a friend's phone

Talking about technology

- Showing off a new purchase
- Buying a new phone
- Talking about an ad

Q: What other situations can you think of? Let's think and talk some more!

9 Fun Facts

Trends in Technology

Did you know?

» People who use phones and tablets to access the Internet will outnumber those who use a PC by 2015.

» 90% of mobile Internet searches lead to action, and 50% lead to a purchase.

» 80% of smartphone owners use their device in stores to shop.

» 60% of Internet users expect a website to load in less than three seconds.

» 100 hours of videos are uploaded to YouTube every minute.

» 93% of marketers are using social media for business.

» The personal cloud is gradually replacing the PC as the location where individuals keep their personal content.

» 82% of companies saved money when they moved to the cloud.

» 2.5 billion gigabytes of data are created every day. That number doubles every month.

» Apps generated $25 billion in revenue in 2013.

Question

① Which statistics are surprising? Which are expected? Why?

② Of the technologies mentioned, what do you use? How do you find it?

③ What are some trends you expect in the next five to ten years? Explain.

Review and Sneak Peek

Calling

_____
_____
_____
_____

Sneak Peek

01.
Do you ever leave messages for other people? What about?

02.
When might you need to leave a message?

| 58 | Pre Get Up To Speed 2

Lesson 10

Can I leave a message?

Learning Objectives :
After studying this lesson, you should be able to...

☑ leave and take down a message from a telephone call

☑ use modal verbs to discuss plans and leave messages

1 Getting Started

A | **Look at the picture and describe what you can see.**

B | **Read the questions below and discuss with your partner.**

① How many phone calls do you make or receive each day? Who do you usually call?

② What are some things you should remember when leaving a message?

Practice the tongue twister with your partner.
Who can say it faster?

» Did Peter Piper pick a peck of pickled peppers? If Peter Piper picked a peck of pickled peppers, where's the peck of pickled peppers Peter Piper picked?

Lesson.10 Can I leave a message? | 59

2 Vocatree

Look at the words given below, brainstorm the synonyms and antonyms for the words.

Synonym ◆ Soon ◆ Antonym

Synonym ◆ Unavailable ◆ Antonym

3 Sentence Building

Complete the sentences by filling in the blanks. Refer to the grammar note note on the right.

1. I will _____ go to the party. I wouldn't want to miss it.
2. If I _____ time, I'll come and visit.
3. She's not sure when she _____ finish. She'll call you later.
4. Tell her I _____ be able to come early, but I don't know yet.
5. I'm so sorry, but I _____ have to cancel. I might have to stay late tonight.
6. She _____ let you know about the trip as soon as possible.
7. Your mother said to _____ you that she will work late.
8. I'm sorry, but I can't go to the movie. I _____ work late tonight.

Grammar Note

Modal Verbs

» I'm not sure what I'll do tonight. I **may** see a movie.
» He said to tell you he **will definitely** come.
» If she has time, she **might** call you back after lunch.
» Tell her I **may** come to see her in the morning.

» Mr. Smith **will** call you back later tonight.
» I **might** come by the office around 5:00.
» I **will** let her know you called right away.
» If the meeting finishes early, I **will** go home early.

4 Dialogue Practice

Arianna	:	Hello, Prime Tech. Arianna speaking.
Ryan	:	Hi, Arianna. May I speak with Bill Smith?
Arianna	:	He's in a meeting right now.
Ryan	:	Could I leave a message for him?
Arianna	:	Yes, of course.
Ryan	:	Could you have him call me back when he gets in?
Arianna	:	Yes. Anything else?
Ryan	:	Please tell him that I have a question about my account.
Arianna	:	Could I have your contact information?

Comprehension Questions

1. Why can't Ryan talk to Bill Smith?
2. What will Ryan say next?
3. What other information might Arianna need for the message?

5 Story Board

Look at the situation and complete the conversation.

Situation.01

Could I speak to Mr. Jones?

Situation.02

May I leave a message for Janet?

6 Comprehensive Listening

Listen to the dialogue and answer the questions.

A Circle True or False

- The woman left a message for Gloria.   True / False
- Terry is eating something now.   True / False
- The woman wants to leave a message.   True / False
- The man wrote down the message.   True / False

B Read each question and write full sentence responses.

- Who made the phone call?

- Who is the message for?

- What message does the woman leave?

- When will the man give Terry the message?

7 Speaking Patterns

Practice using the patterns below with a partner.

Could I leave a message for…?

- » Could I leave a message for Mr. Jones?
- » Could I leave a message for the doctor?
- » Could I leave a message for my wife?

Could you have him call me back when…?

- » Could you have him call me back when his meeting finishes?
- » Could you have him call me back when he comes back?
- » Could you have him call me back when he has time?

Please tell her (him)….

- » Please tell her I'll call back later.
- » Please tell him to call me back.
- » Please tell her I need to talk.

Common Mistakes

What is correct?
Read the sentences and circle the correct answer.
Check the explanations at the back of the book.

01.
New York is far from London. / New York is a long way from London.

02.
My school is 10 minutes from the shop. / My school is 10 minutes far away from the shop.

03.
You should take the bus; it's too far to walk. / You should take the bus; it's too long to walk.

8 Situational Use

What are some things you might say in each situation?

Q: What other situations can you think of? Let's think and talk some more!

9 Fun Facts

How do you use your phone?

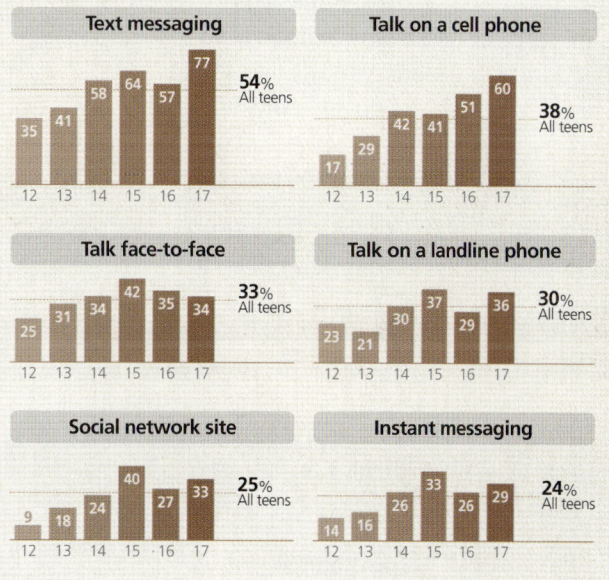

Question

① Explain your mobile usage pattern to your partner. How often do you use your phone? Do you make voice calls more or use text messages?
② Considering your country's situation, how do you find your opinions differ or are the same as the data indicated above?
③ Discuss your favorite ways to communicate with people.

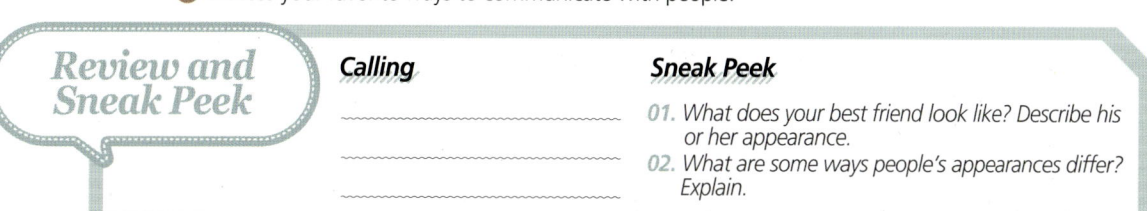

Review and Sneak Peek

Calling
_____
_____
_____

Sneak Peek
01. What does your best friend look like? Describe his or her appearance.
02. What are some ways people's appearances differ? Explain.

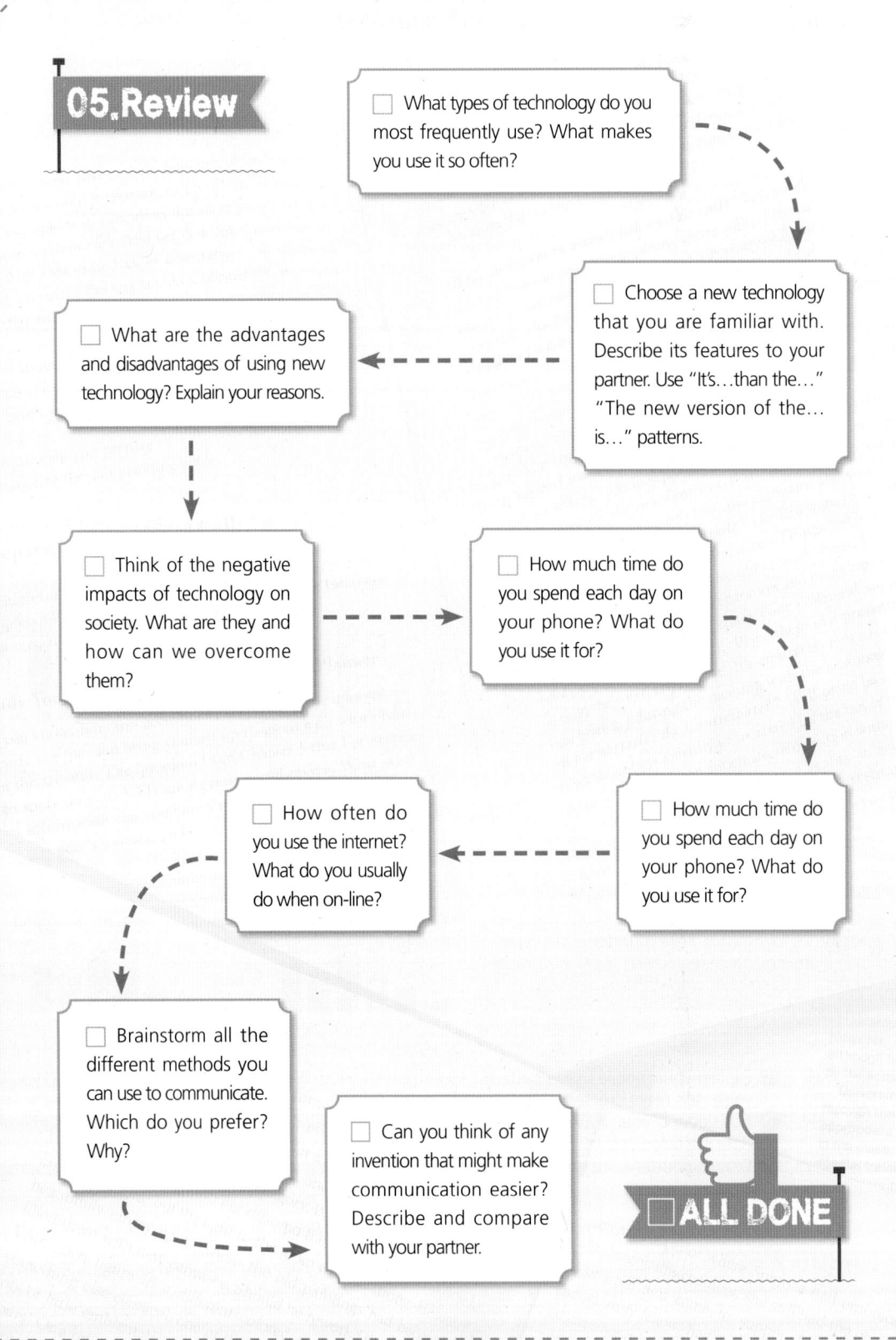

Lesson 11 Describing appearance

Learning Objectives:
After studying this lesson, you should be able to...

- ☑ describe the appearances of different people
- ☑ use adjectives to discuss others' appearance

1 Getting Started

A | Look at the picture and describe what you can see.

Practice the tongue twister with your partner. Who can say it faster?

» A skunk sat on a stump. The stump thought the skunk stunk. The skunk thought the stump stunk. What stunk, the skunk or the stump?

B | Read the questions below and discuss with your partner.

1. What do you look like? Describe yourself to your partner.
2. Do you look like your mother or your father? What about your children? Who do they take after?

2 Vocatree

Look at the words given below, brainstorm the synonyms and antonyms for the words.

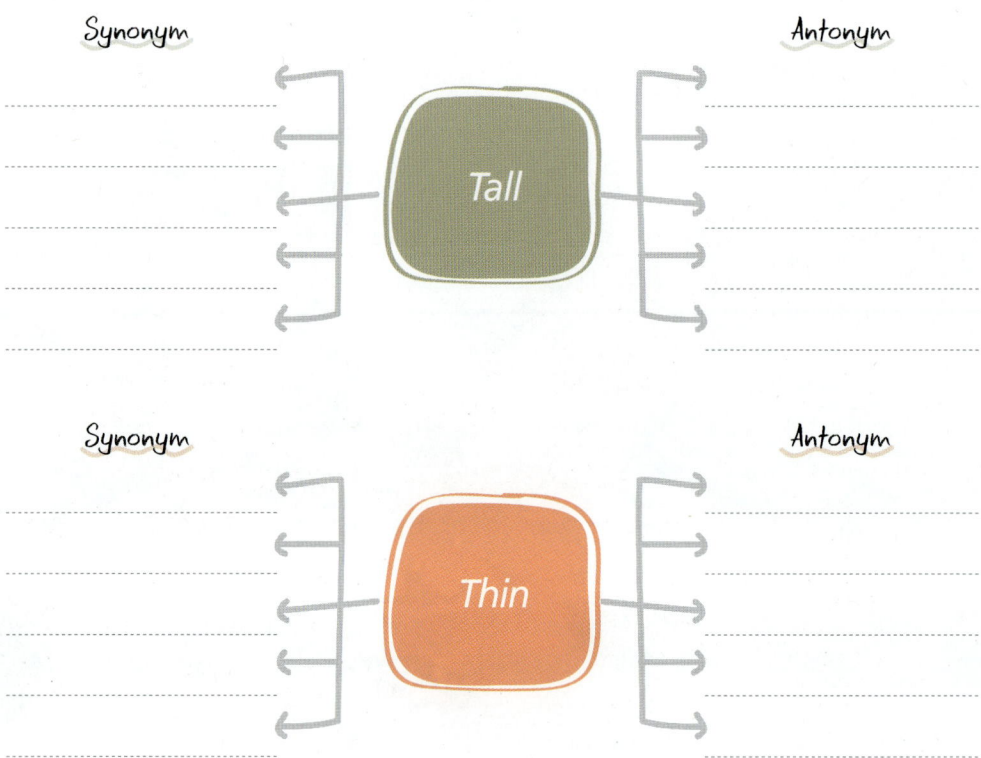

3 Sentence Building

Complete the sentences by filling in the blanks. Refer to the grammar note note on the right.

1. My boss is a very _____ man.

2. I have _____ eyes and black hair.

3. We are similar in height. You are not much _____ than me.

4. Look for a woman with red _____ and freckles.

5. I saw was surprised by how _____ he was in person. I thought he would be shorter.

6. My mother has long _____ hair.

7. Who is the woman with _____ eyes?

8. My hair is naturally _____, but people always think I have a perm.

Grammar Note

Adjectives

» *My sister has **curly red** hair.*
» *I am **tall** and **lean**.*
» *My father is the man with **short brown** hair and freckles.*
» *He is not much **taller** than me.*
» *Who is the **pretty** woman with **long black** hair?*
» *Our teacher is the one with **blue** eyes.*
» *Look for a **tall** man with **short red** hair.*
» *He is a very **handsome** man with **green eyes** and **blond** hair.*

4 Dialogue Practice

Alexander : I can't find Roger. It's so crowded.

Nathan : How would you describe him?

Alexander : He's a little tall and skinny with brown hair.

Nathan : Does he have a beard?

Alexander : No, he doesn't.

Nathan : I don't know. I can't see anyone who fits the description.

Alexander : I see him now! He's the man standing over there by the ticket machine.

Nathan : I can't wait meet him.

Comprehension Questions

1. What are the two men doing?
2. Where do you think the men are meeting?
3. What might happen next?

5 Story Board

Look at the situation and complete the conversation.

Situation.01

I can't find her. What does she look like?

Situation.02

I didn't know you had a brother. What does he look like?

6 Comprehensive Listening

Listen to the dialogue and answer the questions.

A Circle True or False

- The man knows Claire.   True / False
- The man is in a coffee shop.   True / False
- The man finds Claire.   True / False
- Claire is waiting outside the coffee shop.   True / False

B Read each question and write full sentence responses.

- Who is the man looking for?

- Why did the man call the woman?

- What does Claire look like?

- Where is Claire waiting?

7 Speaking Patterns

Practice using the patterns below with a partner.

She's (He's) the…over there.

- » She's the tall woman over there.
- » He's the man with black hair over there.
- » He's the handsome man over there.

She (He) is…and…with…hair.

- » She is short and thin with long hair.
- » He is tall and lean with short hair.
- » She is pale and skinny with gray hair.

How would you describe…?

- » How would you describe him?
- » How would you describe your friend?
- » How would you describe his hair?

Common Mistakes

What is correct?
Read the sentences and circle the correct answer.
Check the explanations at the back of the book.

01
I have been waiting for ten minutes. / I have been waiting since ten minutes.

02
She has been working in France since last winter. / She has been working in France for last winter.

03
They will visit since a week. / They will visit for a week.

| 68 | Pre Get Up To Speed 2

8 Situational Use

What are some things you might say in each situation?

- Seeing an old friend
- Looking at a magazine
- Talking about celebrities
- Talking about appearance
- Complimenting a friend
- At the hair salon
- Describing someone

Q: *What other situations can you think of? Let's think and talk some more!*

9 Fun Facts

Tattoo Prejudice: Do you want to hire people with tattoos?

In the United States, a study conducted by the Journal of the American Academy of Dermatology found that 24% of Americans between 18 and 50 are tattooed; —that's almost one in four and 36% of Americans age 18 to 29 have at least one tattoo. However, discrimination against tattoos still exists.

- **36%** believe tattoos and piercings should be forbidden in the workplace.
- **41%** would not hire someone with visible tattoos and piercings.
- **43%** of companies have a policy concerning visible tattoos and piercings.

N.B. *Women's pierced ears were excluded from these surveys and statistics.*

Question

1. What do you think about a person with tattoos? Discuss.
2. What do you think about the results of the statistics shown above? If you were an HR manager, would you hire a person with a tattoo? Explain your opinion.
3. Do you think first impressions are important? Explain.

Review and Sneak Peek

Calling
_____
_____
_____
_____

Sneak Peek

01.
What characteristics do you look for in a friend? Explain.

02.
Describe your personality. What kind of a person are you?

Lesson.11 Describing appearance

Lesson 12
Describing characteristics

Learning Objectives :
After studying this lesson, you should be able to...

- ☑ describe personality and physical characteristics of people
- ☑ use adjectives and conjunctions to talk about personalities

1 Getting Started

A | Look at the picture and describe what you can see.

Tongue Twisters

Practice the tongue twister with your partner. Who can say it faster?

» Denise sees the fleece. Denise sees the fleas. At least Denise could sneeze and feed and freeze the fleas.

B | Read the questions below and discuss with your partner.

① Talk about your closest friend. What are they like?
② What do you think are attractive characteristics? Why?

2 Vocatree

Look at the words given below, brainstorm the synonyms and antonyms for the words.

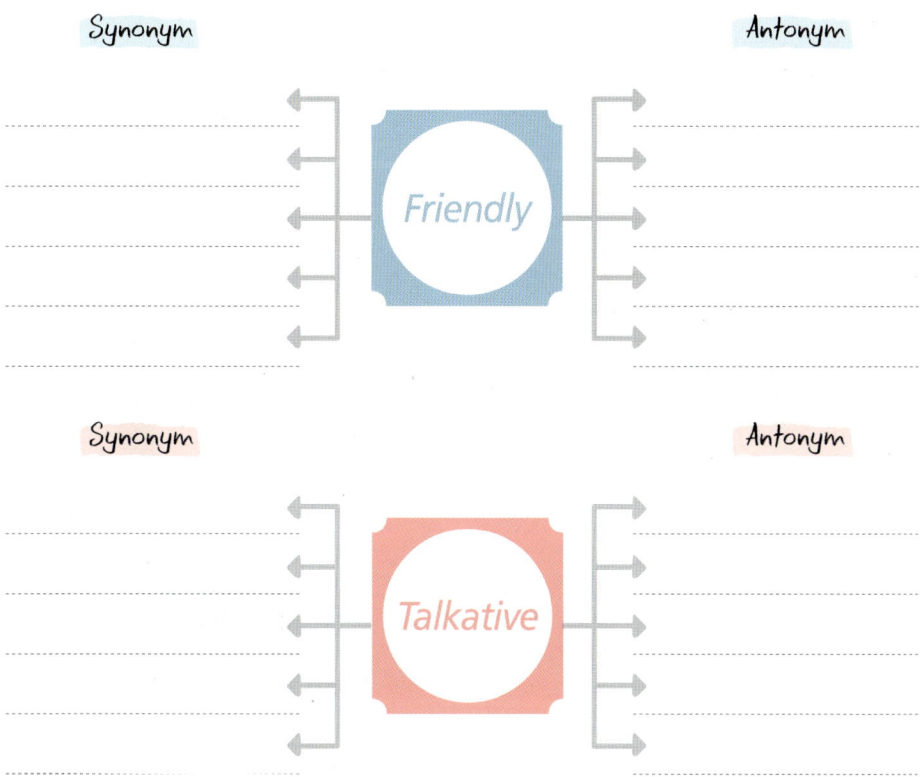

3 Sentence Building

Complete the sentences by filling in the blanks. Refer to the grammar note note on the right.

1. You'_____ even more handsome than I expected.

2. I love your _____ hair.

3. He's a very _____ man.

4. Her children have _____ manners.

5. He has a _____ personality and is very _____.

6. You'_____ got very nice skin.

7. My sister's a very _____ woman.

8. We'_____ both got curly hair and green eyes.

Grammar Note

Adjectives and Conjunctions

» *She's a little **short**, but very **attractive**.*
» *My father's a **good-looking** man.*
» *You're very **tall**!*
» *She's lucky to have such lovely **hair**.*

» *My friend's a little **loud**, but very **funny**.*
» *She's got a **wonderful** personality.*
» *My mother's got **very clear** skin.*
» *You've got **beautiful** manners.*

Lesson.12 Describing characteristics | 71

4 Dialogue Practice

Nora : Did you enjoy meeting Diane last night?

Jack : Yes, she's a very nice woman.

Nora : What did you think of her personality?

Jack : I'd describe her as a very friendly person.

Nora : Yes, she is a very outgoing woman. She has a bright personality.

Jack : I hope that I can meet her again soon.

Nora : I think she'll be at Harry's party next week.

Jack : Are you going, too?

Comprehension Questions

1. Who are the two talking about?
2. What might Nora and Diane's relationship be?
3. What will the two talk about next?

5 Story Board

Look at the situation and complete the conversation.

Situation.01

What kind of a person is your boss?

Situation.02

Tell me more about your parents.

6 Comprehensive Listening

Listen to the dialogue and answer the questions.

A. Circle True or False

- The couple planned to have dinner with Bill.	True / False
- Bill is a little shy.	True / False
- Bill has a great sense of humor.	True / False
- The man thinks Bill is very energetic.	True / False

B. Read each question and write full sentence responses.

- Who is going to dinner?

- What is Bill's personality like?

- What does the woman think of Bill?

- When will they have dinner?

7 Speaking Patterns

Practice using the patterns below with a partner.

She's (He's) a very…woman (man).

- » She's a very friendly woman.
- » He's a very quiet man.
- » She's a very outgoing woman.

…has a(n)…personality.

- » My friend has a wonderful personality.
- » She has an interesting personality.
- » My friend has an energetic personality.

I'd describe her (him) as a…woman (man).

- » I'd describe him as a kind man.
- » I'd describe her as a sensitive woman.
- » I'd describe him as a strong man.

Common Mistakes

What is correct?
Read the sentences and circle the correct answer.
Check the explanations at the back of the book.

01
There is not much milk left. / There is not many milk left.

02
We picked too much strawberries on the farm. / We picked too many strawberries on the farm.

03
How much brothers do you have? / How many brothers do you have?

Lesson.12 Describing characteristics

8 Situational Use

What are some things you might say in each situation?

- Complaining about a boss
- Telling a story
- On a blind date
- Talking about characteristics
- Taking about a friend
- Interviewing for a job
- Introducing two people

Q: *What other situations can you think of? Let's think and talk some more!*

9 Fun Facts

Define a Great Leader

A great leader can be defined with various terms.

Honesty, focus, passion, respect, excellent persuasion abilities, confidence, clarity, care, integrity, compassion, shared vision and actions, engagement, celebration, humility, empowering, collaborative, communicative, fearlessness, genuine, self-awareness, leverage team strengths, supportive.

In the modern world of dynamic international interaction, becoming a global leader is also important. Skills that were most commonly required by global leaders included *overseas experience, deep self-awareness, sensitivity to cultural diversity, humility, lifelong curiosity, cautious honesty, global strategic thinking, patiently impatient, well-spoken, good negotiator, and presence.*

Question

1. Select five words from the list above to create your own definition of a great leader and compare with your classmates.

2. Cultural differences have an impact on what is described as an ideal leader's characteristics. What are the favored characteristics of a leader in your country? How do they compare your answer for Question 1?

3. Do you think leadership characteristics can be learned, or are they natural talents?

Review and Sneak Peek

Calling

_____
_____
_____
_____

Sneak Peek

01.
What do you regret about the past?

02.
Is there anything that you wish you had done differently today?

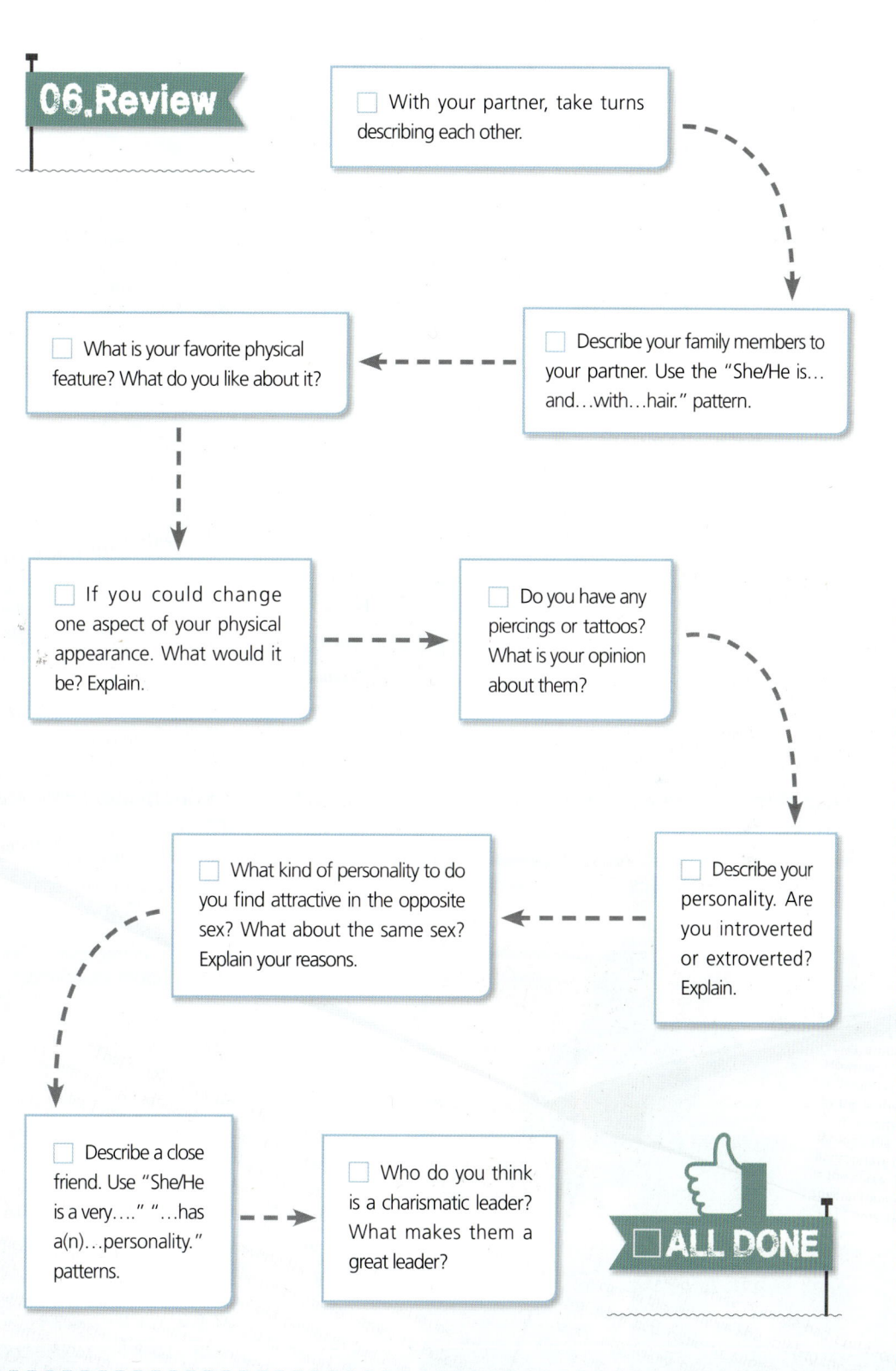

Lesson 13
I should have…

Learning Objectives :
After studying this lesson, you should be able to…

☑ express regrets about the past

☑ use the 3rd conditional to discuss things you wish had gone differently

1 Getting Started

A | Look at the picture and describe what you can see.

B | Read the questions below and discuss with your partner.

❶ Have you ever regretted doing something or not doing something? What was it?

❷ What do you think is better, trying and failing or not trying at all? Explain your choice.

Practice the tongue twister with your partner. Who can say it faster?

» Luke Luck likes lakes. Luke's duck likes lakes. Luke Luck licks lakes. Luck's duck licks lakes. Duck takes licks in lakes Luke Luck likes. Luke Luck takes licks in lakes duck likes.

2 Vocatree

Look at the words given below, brainstorm the synonyms and antonyms for the words.

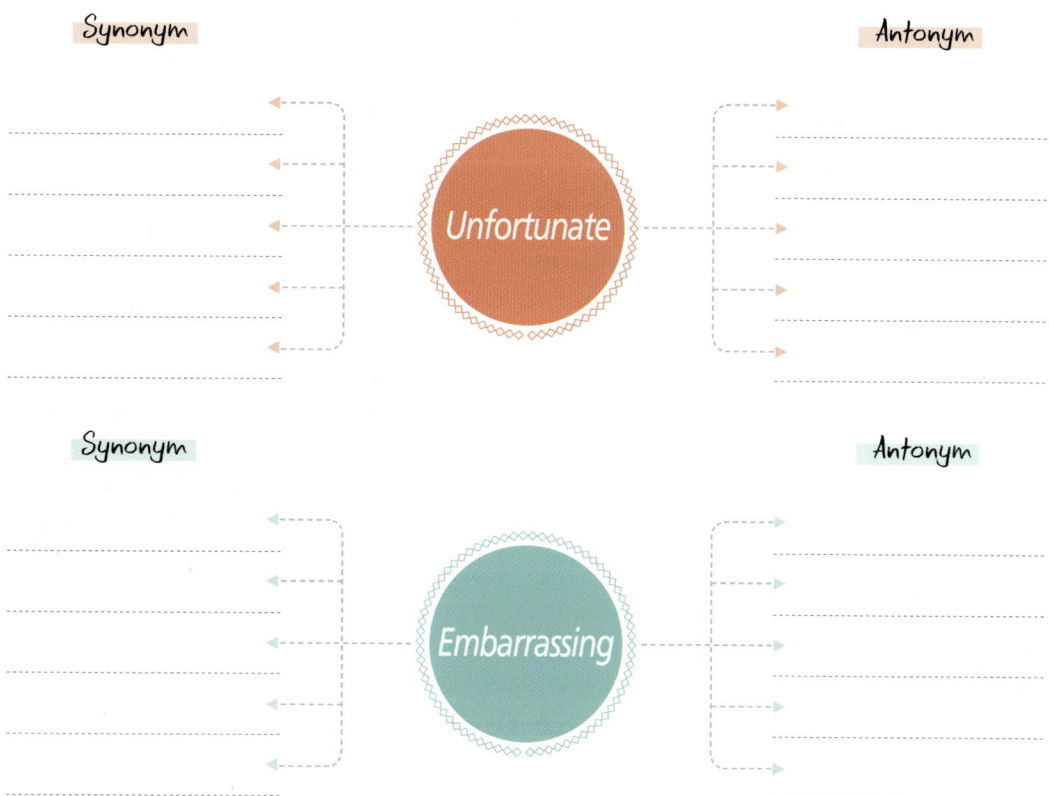

3 Sentence Building

Complete the sentences by filling in the blanks.
Refer to the grammar note note on the right.

1. If she _____ come sooner, we would have had lunch.
2. If I had brought my wallet, I would _____ bought that dress.
3. What would you have done if she _____ found your phone?
4. If I had _____ you were sick, I would have visited.
5. If I hadn't overslept, I _____ have been late.
6. If I had known you needed a ride, I would _____ driven you.
7. If _____ hadn't skipped school, he wouldn't have been in trouble.
8. _____ would have happed if you missed the bus?

Grammar Note

3rd Conditional "If I had…"

» If I **hadn't quit** school, I **would be finished** by now.
» If he **had done** his laundry, he **would have** clean clothes.
» If she **had taken** the bus, she **wouldn't have been** late.
» What **would** you **have done** if I **hadn't been** there to help?

» If I **had gone** home sooner I **wouldn't be** so tired.
» If I **hadn't gone** on vacation, I **w.ould have** more money.
» If she **had prepared** for the test, she **wouldn't have** failed.
» If I **hadn't lost** my wallet, I **would have** your number.

Lesson.13 I should have… | 77

4 Dialogue Practice

Harper : Thank you so much for the ride.

Natalie : What would you have done if I hadn't been there to help?

Harper : I don't know. I wish I hadn't forgotten my wallet, or I would have taken a taxi.

Natalie : Missing the last bus was unfortunate.

Harper : I know. I shouldn't have waited so late.

Natalie : It's okay. You can call me anytime.

Harper : You're a really great friend.

Natalie : No problem. Try to leave for the bus earlier next time.

Comprehension Questions

1. What did Harper forget?
2. What might have been Harper's problem?
3. What might happen next?

5 Story Board

Look at the situation and complete the conversation.

Situation.01

What's the matter? You look upset.

Situation.02

Is everything okay? You're really late.

6 Comprehensive Listening

Listen to the dialogue and answer the questions.

A Circle True or False

- The couple is married.   True / False
- The family went somewhere for summer vacation.   True / False
- The kids didn't have fun at home.   True / False
- The woman regrets staying home.   True / False

B Read each question and write full sentence responses.

- What is the couple talking about?

- Why did the woman think it was her fault?

- Why did the man think it was his fault?

- Why did the woman think the children enjoyed their vacation?

7 Speaking Patterns

Practice using the patterns below with a partner.

…ing…was unfortunate.

- » Quitting school was unfortunate.
- » Losing my wallet was unfortunate.
- » Forgetting my phone was unfortunate.

I wish I hadn't….

- » I wish I hadn't been late.
- » I wish I hadn't taken the bus.
- » I wish I hadn't cancelled vacation.

I shouldn't have….

- » I shouldn't have called so late.
- » I shouldn't have driven here.
- » I shouldn't have bought this jacket.

Common Mistakes

What is correct?
Read the sentences and circle the correct answer.
Check the explanations at the back of the book.

01.
The waiter asked if we were all together. / The waiter asked if we were altogether.

02.
The boy played the piano less and less and eventually stopped all together. / The boy played the piano less and less and eventually stopped altogether.

03.
All together, I have worked for this company for 15 years. / Altogether, I have worked for this company for 15 years.

8 Situational Use

What are some things you might say in each situation?

- On a rainy day
- Meeting an old friend
- After losing money
- After vacation
- At a school reunion
- When you get lost

Talking about regrets

Q: *What other situations can you think of? Let's think and talk some more!*

9 Fun Facts

Do you want to meet your lost love?

We all have regrets, but research suggests the most common regret involves a lost romantic opportunity. Researchers at Northwestern University and the University of Illinois at Urbana-Champaign collected data from 370 adults. The most common regret involved romance, with nearly one in five respondents telling a story of a missed love connection. The second most common regret involved family issues, with 16% of respondents expressing regret about a family controversy or having been unkind to a sibling as a child. Other top regrets involved *education (13%), career (12%), money issues (10%), parenting mistakes (9%) and health regrets (6%)*.

Question

① Do you agree or disagree with the results of the survey above? Why?

② Talk about your biggest regret and what you would have done differently if you had another chance.

③ What is a solution to having regrets? Share your ideas.

Review and Sneak Peek

Calling
_____
_____
_____
_____

Sneak Peek

01.
What is your favorite holiday? Why?

02.
How do you prepare for a birthday or other special occasion?

Lesson

14 Special occasions

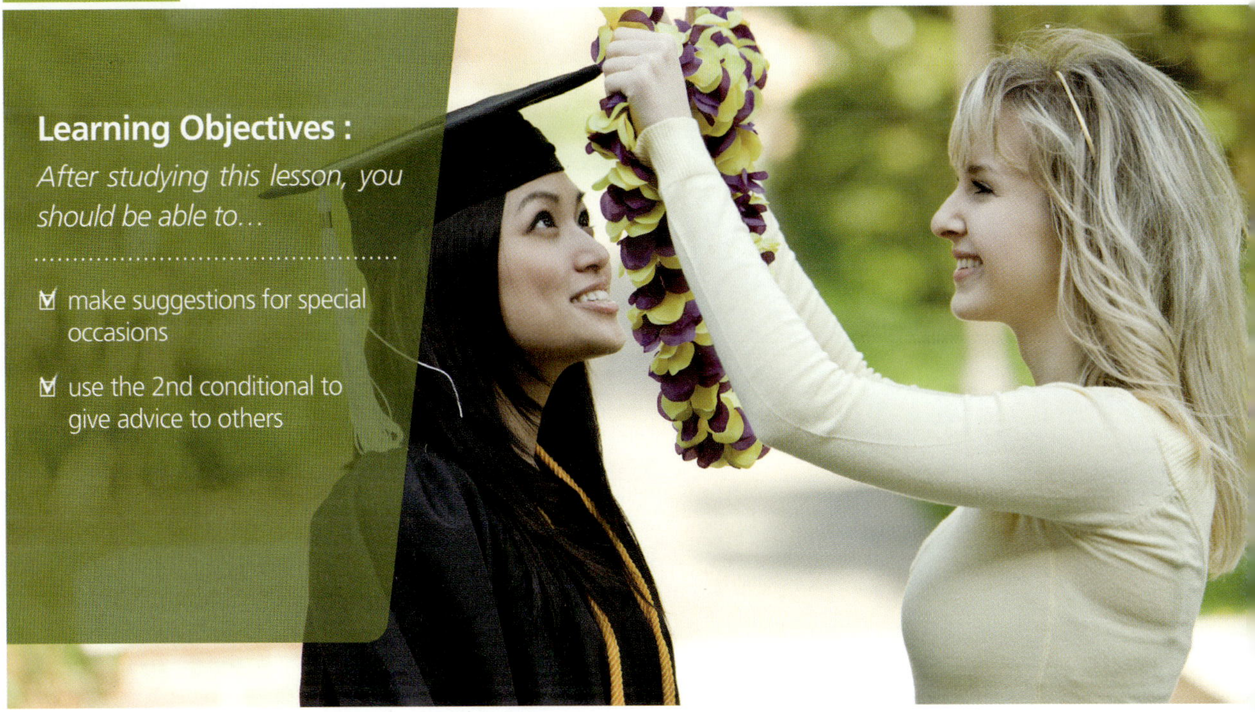

Learning Objectives :

After studying this lesson, you should be able to...

- ☑ make suggestions for special occasions
- ☑ use the 2nd conditional to give advice to others

1 Getting Started

A | Look at the picture and describe what you can see.

Tongue Twisters

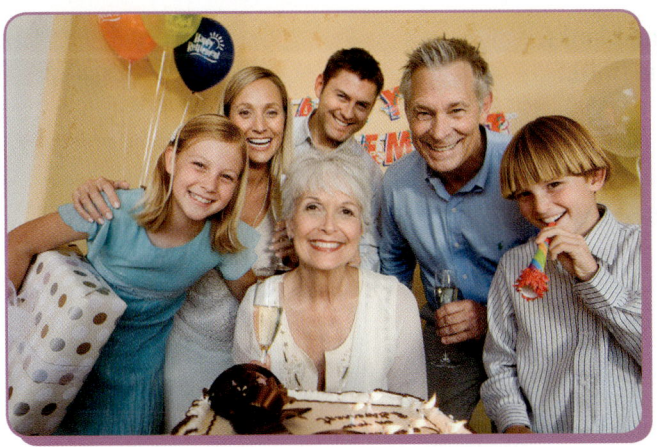

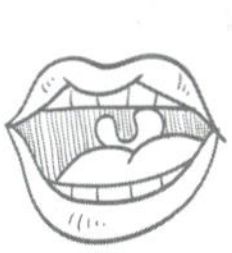

Practice the tongue twister with your partner.
Who can say it faster?

» If colored caterpillars could change their colors constantly, could they keep their colored coat colored properly?

B | Read the questions below and discuss with your partner.

1. What are some special occasions or anniversaries you try to remember?
2. How do you celebrate on special occasions? What do you do?

2 Vocatree

Look at the words given below, brainstorm the synonyms and antonyms for the words.

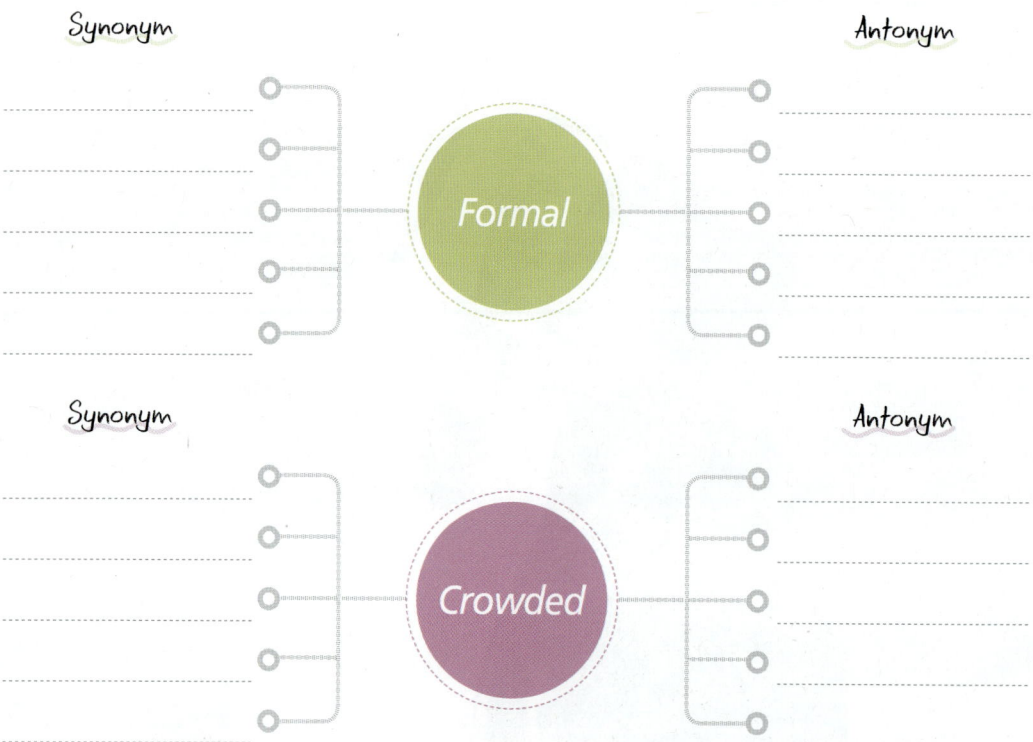

3 Sentence Building

Complete the sentences by filling in the blanks. Refer to the grammar note note on the right.

1. She _____ have finished eating by now if she had just cooked.

2. If you would have called sooner, I would have been able to _____ dinner.

3. If he would have _____ a reservation in advance, we would have a table.

4. If I had his phone number, I would _____ him.

5. He would cook _____ if he didn't have to work.

6. If I were _____, I would ask for help.

7. My boss would have announced the meeting sooner if he _____ so busy.

8. She would _____ cookies for the guests if the oven weren't broken.

Grammar Note

2nd Conditional "If I were..."

» If I **were** you, I **would order** Chinese food.
» If I **had** a party, I **would have** it at the Green Hotel.
» She **would come** earlier if she **didn't have** to work.
» If there **were** more time, I **would bake** a cake.

» I **wouldn't have** my wedding there if I **were** you.
» He **would buy** it himself if he **weren't** so busy.
» If I **were** him, I **would go** home for Christmas.
» I **would have booked** in advance if I **were** you.

4 🎙️ Dialogue Practice

Cooper : You're getting married next year, right?

Samantha : Yes, in April.

Cooper : Have you picked a place to have your wedding yet?

Samantha : I wish I had a plan, but I don't have the time to look at anywhere.

Cooper : If I had the money, I'd have it in a hotel downtown.

Samantha : That would be nice. If I had time, I would probably look into that.

Cooper : What would you do if you had unlimited money for your wedding?

Samantha : I'd have to think about that….

Comprehension Questions

1. Why doesn't Samantha have a plan for her wedding yet?
2. What might their relationship be?
3. What might Samantha want?

5 Story Board

Look at the situation and complete the conversation.

Situation.01

I'm not sure what to do for my birthday party…. I only turn 30 once…

Situation.02

What should I get my wife for her Christmas present? She's so picky.

Lesson.14 Special occasions | 83

6 Comprehensive Listening

Listen to the dialogue and answer the questions.

A | Circle True or False

- The man and woman are planning a vacation. —— True / False
- The man wants to go to the Maldives. —— True / False
- The woman went to Europe on her last vacation. —— True / False
- The man doesn't have the money to go to the Maldives. —— True / False

B | Read the following questions and write full sentence responses.

- What would the man want to do if he had more vacation?

- What does the man ask the woman?

- What does the woman want to do?

- What would you do if you had another week of vacation?

7 Speaking Patterns

Practice using the patterns below with a partner.

If I had the money, I would….
- If I had the money, I would quit my job.
- If I had the money, I would buy a car.
- If I had the money, I would buy a new television.

If I had time, I would….
- If I had time, I would visit my mother.
- If I had time, I would go home before dinner.
- If I had time, I would take a vacation.

What would you do if you…?
- What would you do if you got a promotion?
- What would you do if you had more vacation?
- What would you do if you won the lottery?

Common Mistakes

What is correct?
Read the sentences and circle the correct answer.
Check the explanations at the back of the book.

01 Every day I go for a run in the park. / Everyday I go for a run in the park.

02 Being late is an everyday event for him. / Being late is an every day event for him.

03 He wants to eat pizza everyday. / He wants to eat pizza every day.

8 Situational Use

What are some things you might say in each situation?

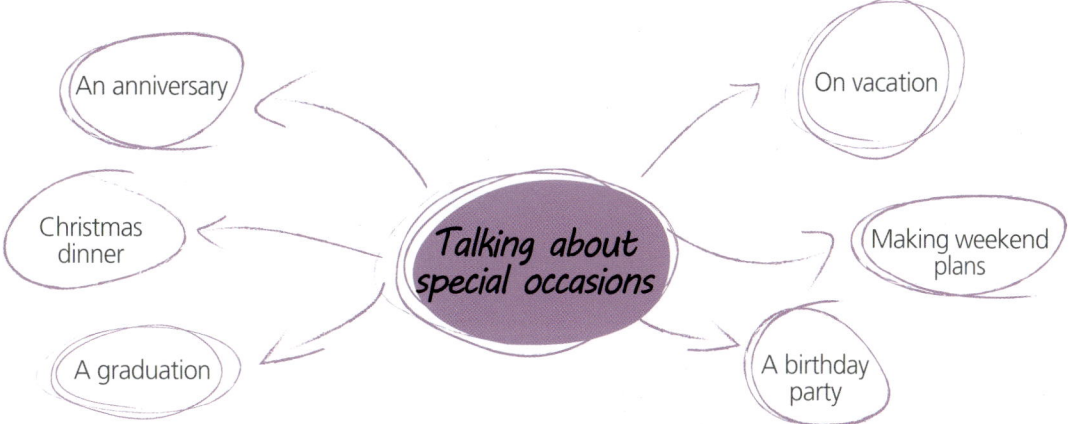

Q: *What other situations can you think of? Let's think and talk some more!*

9 Fun Facts

Birthday Traditions around the world

Each one of us has various special occasions to celebrate throughout the year; birthdays, weddings, anniversaries, graduations, retirements and baptisms are just a few. Among them, birthdays are perhaps the most commonly celebrated. Here are some birthday traditions :

Ireland The birthday child is lifted upside down and "bumped" on the floor for good luck. The number of bumps given is the age of the child plus one for extra good luck.

Australia Children eat a dish called "Fairy Bread," buttered bread covered with tiny sprinkles known as "hundreds and thousands."

India Children receive and wear new clothes on their birthday.

Mexico When a birthday child is having a party with friends, a piñata, an animal-shaped balloon filled with candies, toys and coins, is hanging outside the backyard and will be broken as part of the celebration.

Israel The birthday child wears a crown made from leaves or flowers and sits in a chair decorated in streamers while guests dance around the chair singing. The chair with the child sitting in it is lifted up by his or her parents.

Review and Sneak Peek

Calling

Sneak Peek

01.
What is your ideal holiday?

02.
What plans do you have for the next holiday?

Question

① How do you celebrate your birthday?

② Talk about your best birthday present or best birthday celebration occasion.

③ What are the birthday traditions in your country? Explain how it differs from the list above.

07. Review

- ☐ List three things that you regularly forget to do. Why do you think you forget?

- ☐ In the last week have you done anything that you regret? Use "I wish I hadn't…" "I shouldn't have…" patterns.

- ☐ Do you think that having some form of regret is healthy? Explain your reasons.

- ☐ What are your biggest regrets? How do you try to overcome them?

- ☐ What is the most important annual event that you celebrate? Why?

- ☐ Is there anything special you wish to do for an upcoming anniversary or event?

- ☐ Use "If I had the money, I would…" "If I had the time, I would…" patterns to describe the perfect vacation.

- ☐ What is your most memorable party or celebration? Explain what happened.

- ☐ Describe a traditional or public holiday that your country celebrates. What are the origins and traditions?

☐ **ALL DONE**

Lesson 15
Holiday plans

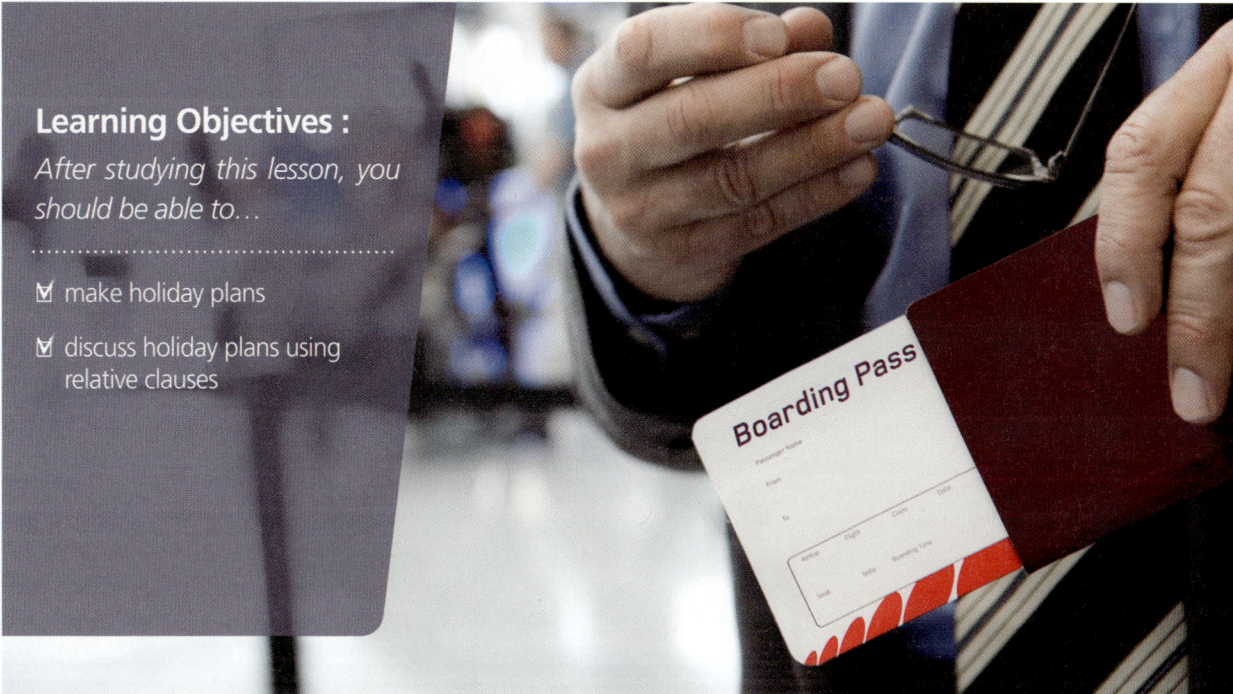

Learning Objectives :
After studying this lesson, you should be able to…

☑ make holiday plans

☑ discuss holiday plans using relative clauses

1 Getting Started

A | Look at the picture and describe what you can see.

Practice the tongue twister with your partner. Who can say it faster?

» As he gobbled the cakes on his plate, the greedy ape said as he ate, the "The greener green grapes are, the keener keen apes are to gobble green grape cakes, they're. They're great!"

B | Read the questions below and discuss with your partner.

1. When was your last holiday? What did you do?
2. Do you enjoy making holiday plans? Why or why not?

2 Vocatree

Look at the words given below, brainstorm the synonyms and antonyms for the words.

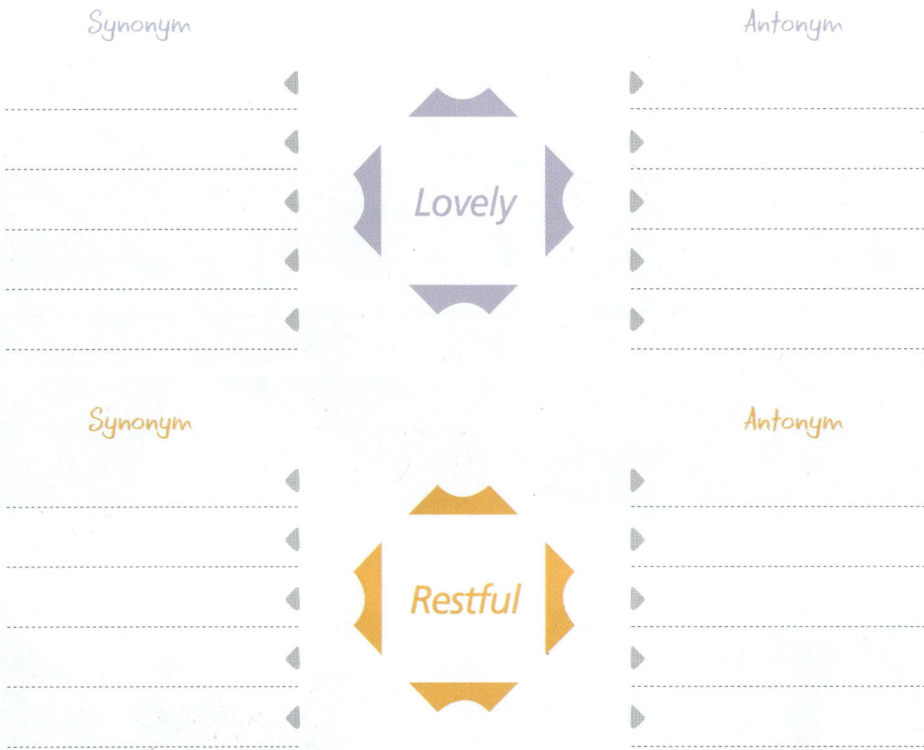

3 Sentence Building

**Complete the sentences by filling in the blanks.
Refer to the grammar note note on the right.**

1. The party _____ our neighbor is having starts at 9:00.

2. The restaurant _____ we wanted to go was closed for Christmas.

3. The grocery _____ that is near us closed today.

4. I made plans to meet some friends _____ I know from the gym.

5. The movie _____ we plan to see has good reviews.

6. The resort _____ we made a reservation is supposed to be great.

7. There is my friend _____ is waiting for me.

8. I've never been to a celebration _____ was so big.

Grammar Note

Relative Clauses

» *This is the resort* **where we will be going**.
» *Here is my friend* **who I'm meeting for dinner**.
» *My friend* **who planned to visit** had to work on the holiday.
» *The festival* **that will be downtown** will start at 9:00.
» *I made plans with my friend* **whom I know from college**.
» *The children* **who live in our neighborhood** will come to the Christmas party.
» *The woman* **who runs the restaurant** took the day off.
» *The store* **that is next door** closed for the holiday.

4 Dialogue Practice

Sebastian	:	Are you planning on taking a vacation for the holidays?
Molly	:	No, I'm just going to hang out at home while I'm off work.
Sebastian	:	That sounds very restful.
Molly	:	What are you doing for New Year's Eve?
Sebastian	:	My cousin is having a big party.
Molly	:	That sounds fun.
Sebastian	:	You should come, too.
Molly	:	Are you sure? I'd hate to invite myself along.

Comprehension Questions

1. What will Molly be doing for the holiday?
2. What season do you think the conversation is taking place?
3. What might they talk about next?

5 Story Board

Look at the situation and complete the conversation.

Situation.01

I almost forgot tomorrow is a holiday. Any special plans?

Situation.02

Only two more days until Christmas…What are you planning on doing for the holidays?

6 Comprehensive Listening

Listen to the dialogue and answer the questions.

A Circle True or False

- The woman will be busy with work.　　　　　True / False
- The woman's parents live far away.　　　　　True / False
- The woman will visit her hometown.　　　　　True / False
- There is a holiday weekend soon.　　　　　　True / False

B Read the following questions and write full sentence responses.

- What is the conversation about?

- Why isn't the man going anywhere?

- Where do the woman's parents live?

- What kind of work does the man have to do?

---

7 Speaking Patterns

Practice using the patterns below with a partner.

What are you doing for…?

- » What are you doing for New Year's?
- » What are you doing for your Christmas vacation?
- » What are you doing for Thanksgiving?

Are you planning on…for the holidays?

- » Are you planning on going home for the holidays?
- » Are you planning on taking a vacation for the holidays?
- » Are you planning on visiting your parents for the holidays?

I'm going to…while I'm off work.

- » I'm going to take a rest while I'm off work.
- » I'm going to visit my parents while I'm off work.
- » I'm going to clean my house while I'm off work.

Common Mistakes

What is correct?
Read the sentences and circle the correct answer. Check the explanations at the back of the book.

01.
Playing sports makes me feel exciting. / Playing sports makes me feel excited.

02.
The children were excited to bake cookies. / The children were exciting to bake cookies.

03.
I think that this movie is very exciting. / I think that this movie is very excited.

8 Situational Use

What are some things you might say in each situation?

- Calling a relative
- Planning a party
- Cancelling an appointment
- Making reservations
- Calling a friend
- At the airport

Talking about holiday plans

Q: What other situations can you think of? Let's think and talk some more!

9 Fun Facts

How do you plan for your holidays?

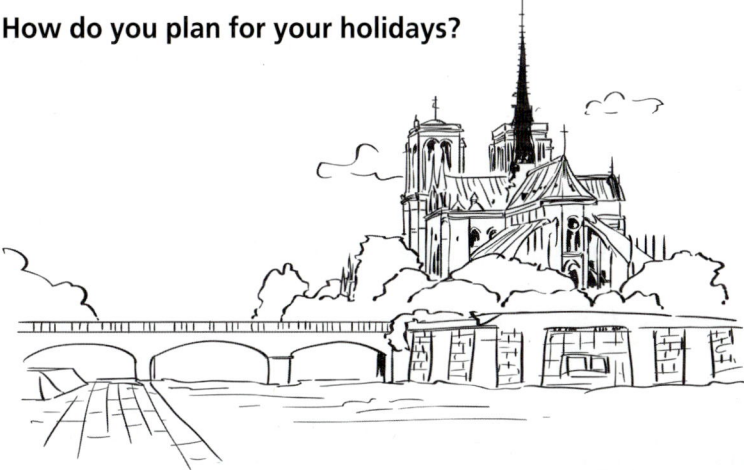

Research conducted in the UK shows changes in travelers' preferences in recent years. Travelers are now seeking for more flexible schedules and benefits. Travel preferences moved from package tours to individual-focused and tailor-made experiences. In difficult economic times, travelers preferred to plan ahead and book earlier to secure cheaper travel deals. Longer holidays and multi-destination trips also increased.

Question

1. Are the trends in travel preferences surprising? Why or why not?
2. What do you usually consider the most when you are planning for a holiday? Compare with your partner.
3. Where do you want to go for your next holiday trip? Explain where you want to go and why.

Review and Sneak Peek

Calling
_____
_____
_____

Sneak Peek

01.
What are your plans for the future?

02.
What do you think you will be doing this time next year?

Lesson.15 Holiday plans | 91

Lesson 16 — Getting away

Learning Objectives :
After studying this lesson, you should be able to...

- ☑ discuss the future
- ☑ tell others about future plans using gerunds

1 Getting Started

A | Look at the picture and describe what you can see.

B | Read the questions below and discuss with your partner.

1. How do you feel when you think about the future? Why?
2. Talk about your five-year and ten-year plan. Where do you see yourself then?

Practice the tongue twister with your partner. Who can say it faster?

» How much dew does a dewdrop drop if dewdrops do drop dew? They do drop. They do as do dewdrops drop if dewdrops do drop dew.

2 Vocatree

Look at the words given below, brainstorm the synonyms and antonyms for the words.

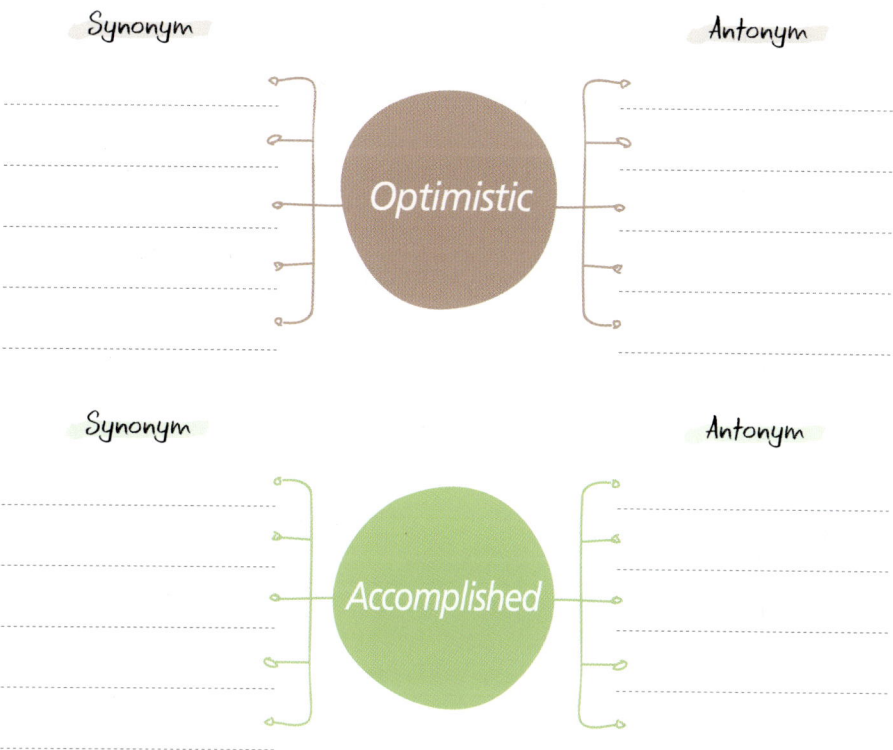

3 Sentence Building

Complete the sentences by filling in the blanks. Refer to the grammar note note on the right.

1. I'm _____ forward to the holiday.

2. My mother is looking _____ to our visit.

3. We _____ looking forward to watching the movie.

4. He is looking forward to _____ at that restaurant.

5. My family is looking forward to _____ on vacation.

6. Our children are _____ forward to the day off from school.

7. _____ am looking forward to seeing your new apartment.

8. She _____ looking forward to meeting her old school friends.

Grammar Note

Future & Gerunds

» *What **are** you **looking forward to seeing** on your trip?*

» *I'm **looking forward to trying** bungee jumping.*

» *She's **looking forward to going** on vacation.*

» *My brother **is looking forward to going** to college.*

» *Are you **looking forward to starting** your new job?*

» *She's **looking forward to having** a break from work.*

» *I'm **looking forward to getting** a haircut.*

» *My family is **looking forward to attending** your party.*

Lesson.16 Getting away | 93

4 Dialogue Practice

Keira	: Are you ready for your new job?
Alyssa	: Yes, I'm really excited.
Keira	: You aren't worried about changing careers?
Alyssa	: No, I'm optimistic about the opportunity.
Keira	: That's a good way to think about it.
Alyssa	: Yes, I'm looking forward to doing something different.
Keira	: You won't miss your students?
Alyssa	: No, I'm ready to work with adults again.

Comprehension Questions

1. What are the two women discussing?
2. Why might Alyssa be changing jobs?
3. What might Alyssa's current job be?

5 Story Board

Look at the situation and complete the conversation.

Situation.01

What are your plans after you graduate?

Situation.02

What are you going to do over the vacation?

6 Comprehensive Listening

Listen to the dialogue and answer the questions.

A | Circle True or False

- The woman is going on vacation.   *True / False*
- The man will go hiking on his vacation.   *True / False*
- The man and woman are married.   *True / False*
- The man is happy about his upcoming vacation.   *True / False*

B | Read the following questions and write full sentence responses.

- Where is the man going?

  ....

- What is the man optimistic about?

  ....

- How does the woman expect he feels?

  ....

- When will the man leave?

  ....

7 Speaking Patterns

Practice using the patterns below with a partner.

I'm looking forward to....
- I'm looking forward to going back to school.
- I'm looking forward to my new job.
- I'm looking forward to my upcoming vacation.

I'm optimistic about....
- I'm optimistic about my new business.
- I'm optimistic about the change.
- I'm optimistic about taking the exam.

I'm ready to start....
- I'm ready to start my new career.
- I'm ready to start graduate school.
- I'm ready to start my year abroad.

Common Mistakes

What is correct?
Read the sentences and circle the correct answer.
Check the explanations at the back of the book.

01.
As soon as I put on a coat, I will be all ready. / As soon as I put on a coat, I will be already.

02.
She was already at the restaurant. / She was all ready at the restaurant.

03.
They were all ready to order. / They were already to order.

8 Situational Use

What are some things you might say in each situation?

- Planning a career change
- Moving to a new home
- On a job interview
- Discussing plans
- At the travel agent
- With a friend
- Registering for classes

Q: *What other situations can you think of? Let's think and talk some more!*

9 Fun Facts

Are you living your dream?

A study conducted in 2012 with 8,000 US professionals showed that 30% of people were working in the careers they dreamed of as kids. Researchers also showed how people choose their careers. Influential factors were parents' professions, perceived talents, the environment, suggestions by teachers or other influencers, or just opportunities.

Setting up long-term goals and having a goal-oriented focus were useful tools to measure one's progress and continuously motivate him or her to progress toward his or her dream job. One in eight adults said they gave up their childhood dream jobs for more profitable careers whereas two-thirds of US teenagers are willing to give up their dreams for higher paying professions.

 **Question**

1. What was your dream job as a child? Why?
2. Consider your current job. Is it how you saw yourself as a child? If not, what caused the changes?
3. Do you have long-term life plan or goal? Explain.

Review and Sneak Peek

Calling
_____
_____
_____
_____

List three things you learned while studying this book. Share with your partner.

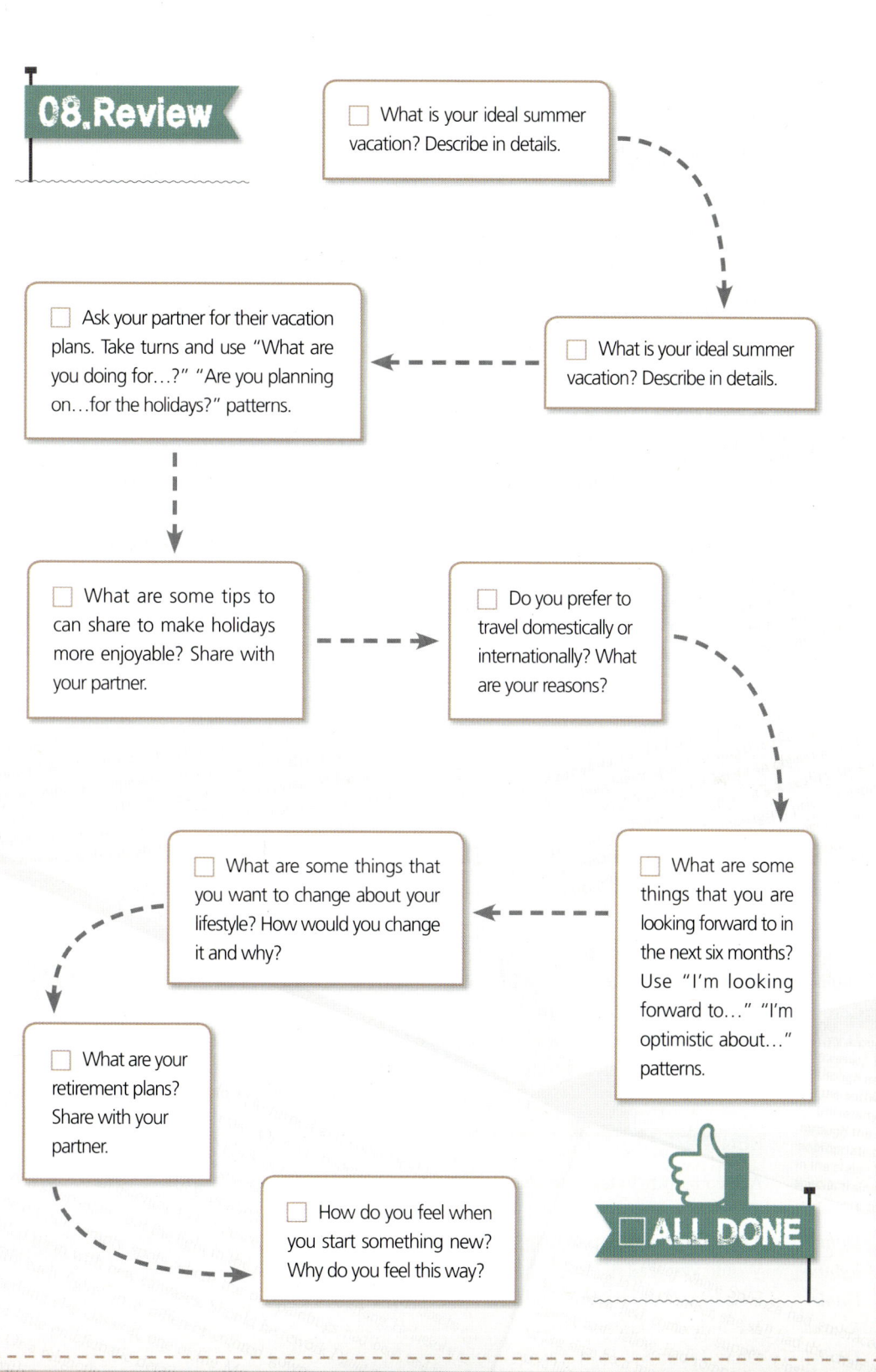

AUDIO SCRIPTS

Lesson.01　Long time no see!

DIALOGUE PRACTICE

Matthew : Hey, Jenny! I haven't seen you since graduation!
Jenny : I've been busy with graduate school. How is work going?
Matthew : I like my new job, but they're transferring me to another office soon.
Jenny : Where are you going?
Matthew : I'm moving to Europe for a year.
Jenny : Europe? Really?
Matthew : I know… It's so far away. I was worried that I wouldn't see you before I left.
Jenny : Do you have time for coffee? We should catch up.

COMPREHENSIVE LISTENING

Megan : Is that you, Ryan? I haven't seen you since I changed jobs.
Ryan : Megan? Hey! How is your new job going?
Megan : It's a little busy, but I like it a lot.
Ryan : That's great to hear. It's good to see you. It's been so long.
Megan : I know. I was worried that you wouldn't recognize me.
Ryan : You should visit the office sometime. Everyone would be happy to see you.
Megan : I might just do that.
Ryan : Here. Let me give you my new number. You should give me a call.

Lesson.02　I'm walking my pet

DIALOGUE PRACTICE

Daniel : Are you ready to go to dinner now?
Corey : I need to walk my dog before we go out.
Daniel : How often do you walk your dog?
Corey : I usually walk it twice a day at the park.
Daniel : Your dog is so cute. I bet walking it is fun.
Corey : It is. You should try it some time.
Daniel : I'd like that. Let me know if you ever need help.
Corey : Okay, how about next month? Would you like to walk my dog for me when I visit my mother?

COMPREHENSIVE LISTENING

Daniel : Are you ready to leave for the party yet?
Joanna : Give me 20 minutes. I need to finish a few more things before we go out.
Daniel : Could I do anything to help?
Joanna : Would you feed my dog for me?
Daniel : Of course. Where's the food?
Joanna : It's under the kitchen sink.
Daniel : Okay. I found it. How much should I give it?
Joanna : Just fill up the red bowl, please.

Lesson.03 Going grocery shopping

DIALOGUE PRACTICE

Sophia : This produce looks very fresh!
Store clerk : It's the freshest in town. We get it all from a local farm.
Sophia : How much for a kilogram of oranges?
Store clerk : They're $4 a kilogram.
Sophia : What about the grapefruit?
Store clerk : They're also $4.
Sophia : Can I mix them? Could you give me half a kilogram of each?
Store clerk : Sure thing. Could I bag that for you?

COMPREHENSIVE LISTENING

Store clerk : What can I get for you?
Kelly : This fish looks very fresh. How much for one?
Store clerk : It's $3 a kilogram. Which one do you want? I'll weigh it.
Kelly : Could you give me the biggest one?
Store clerk : Okay. It's 2 kilograms, so that will be $6.
Kelly : That sounds good.
Store clerk : I'll wrap the fish up for you.
Kelly : May I pay with a card?
Store clerk : Yes, of course.

Lesson.04 Healthy eating

DIALOGUE PRACTICE

Aiden : I feel so tired lately.
Jacob : You should try eating healthier. Vegetables are good for fatigue.
Aiden : Would that really help?
Jacob : Yes, it would be an affordable solution to your problem.
Aiden : How much should I eat?
Jacob : According to the food pyramid, you should eat at least three servings of vegetables a day.
Aiden : I'm going to try to eat a lot more than that.
Jacob : Don't eat too much. Too much of anything isn't good for you.

COMPREHENSIVE LISTENING

Jonathan : What are you drinking?
Agnes : It's carrot juice. I made it fresh, so there's no sugar in it like the juice you buy at stores.
Jonathan : That's very healthy. Too much sugar isn't good for you.
Agnes : Did you know that carrots are really good for your eyes?
Jonathan : My vision has been getting worse…. Do you think carrot juice would help?
Agnes : Yes. You should eat multiple servings of vegetables a day.
Jonathan : Could I try some?
Agnes : I'll get the blender out again.

AUDIO SCRIPTS

Lesson.05 What are you wearing?

DIALOGUE PRACTICE

Emily   : That's a really nice sweater you have on today.
Logan   : Thanks. I bought it yesterday.
Emily   : I need more warm clothes in this weather.
Logan   : Me, too. It's so cold lately.
Emily   : I'm going shopping later. I need a warmer jacket. This one is too light for this weather.
Logan   : We should go shopping together.
Emily   : I'd like that.
Logan   : What time are you going today?

COMPREHENSIVE LISTENING

Kelsey : What are you doing here at the mall? I thought you hated shopping.
Aiden   : I usually do, but I need more summer clothes in this hot weather.
Kelsey : It has been really warm lately.
Aiden   : What do you think of this shirt?
Kelsey : This shirt is too thick for this weather.
Aiden   : I guess you're right. I should buy a new shirt.
Kelsey : Try this one. What size do you need?
Aiden   : I think I need a medium. I should try it on.

Lesson.06 Shopping smart

DIALOGUE PRACTICE

Mia   : This coat is a real bargain, don't you think?
Charlotte : I'm not sure…. It will probably get cheaper. Winter is almost over.
Mia   : I guess so.
Charlotte : Let's look around some more for a better price.
Mia   : Where could I look?
Charlotte : I think it would be cheaper online.
Mia   : Maybe… I really like it though.
Charlotte : You can always buy it later if you can't find it cheaper.

COMPREHENSIVE LISTENING

Royce   : This television is a real bargain.
Esther : It's still a little expensive. Let's look around for a better price.
Royce   : What do you mean? It's so cheap!
Esther : I think it would be cheaper at an electronics market.
Royce   : Maybe… but it might not be.
Esther : We don't really need it after all. We have a good TV now.
Royce   : I guess you are right.
Esther : It would be nicer to have a bigger one, but we should save our money.

Lesson.07   Asking directions

DIALOGUE PRACTICE

Lily : I just realized what time it is…. I'm going to be late to my meeting.
Oliver : Where are you going? I might know a shortcut.
Lily : What's the best way to get to the Butler Building from here?
Oliver : Go straight for three blocks on Riverside Drive and take a right.
Baylor : I think you should try another route. That road is too curvy to drive quickly on.
Lily : What do you recommend?
Baylor : How about down Martin Street?
Oliver : I agree. That might be better….
Lily : I'll try that. Thanks so much!

COMPREHENSIVE LISTENING

Jake : I'm worried I won't get to the airport in time for my flight.
Lynn : Which way are you going?
Jake : I'm taking the expressway.
Lynn : You should try another route. That road is always busy.
Jake : Okay, then, what's the best way to get there?
Lynn : Take the old highway.
Jake : The old highway?
Lynn : Yes, there's never any traffic.

Lesson.08   Taking public transport

DIALOGUE PRACTICE

Hotel Concierge : How may I help you?
Braden : Could you help me get a taxi to the airport?
Hotel Concierge : There's a lot of traffic now, so I think taking the bus from here is more convenient.
Braden : Really? Could you tell me when the next bus leaves?
Hotel Concierge : It leaves every 30 minutes from in front of the hotel. The next one is at 1 p.m.
Braden : Is it expensive?
Hotel Concierge : No, it's only $3. Our city's public transportation system is affordable.
Braden : Can I buy tickets on the bus?

COMPREHENSIVE LISTENING

Steve : Excuse me. Are you looking for something?
Jessica : I'm looking for the subway station.
Steve : It's a little far. Taking the bus from here is more convenient.
Jessica : Could you tell me when the next bus leaves?
Steve : It should come in about five minutes.
Jessica : How much is it?
Steve : It only costs $1. Our city's bus system is very affordable.
Jessica : Thank you for your help.

AUDIO SCRIPTS

Lesson.09 Trending technology

DIALOGUE PRACTICE

Hannah : Did you change phones?
Gavin : Yes, I got a new one last month.
Hannah : Ah … you have the same one as me.
Gavin : I really like it. It's much more compact than the old one.
Hannah : Have you upgraded the operating system yet?
Gavin : No … is it much different than the old one?
Hannah : Not very, but the new version is much quicker.
Gavin : Could you help me update it?

COMPREHENSIVE LISTENING

Stacey : Have you upgraded your phone yet?
Tony : Yes, I did this morning.
Stacey : What do you think?
Tony : My new smartphone is so much faster.
Stacey : How about the software?
Tony : The new version is much quicker. I really like it.
Stacey : Was it expensive?
Tony : Not very. It was worth the cost.
Stacey : Maybe I should upgrade my phone, too.

Lesson.10 Can I leave a message?

DIALOGUE PRACTICE

Arianna : Hello, Prime Tech. Arianna speaking.
Ryan : Hi, Arianna. May I speak with Bill Smith?
Arianna : He's in a meeting right now.
Ryan : Could I leave a message for him?
Arianna : Yes, of course.
Ryan : Could you have him call me back when he gets in?
Arianna : Yes. Anything else?
Ryan : Please tell him that I have a question about my account.
Arianna : Could I have your contact information?

COMPREHENSIVE LISTENING

Sean : Hello.
Gloria : Hi, is Terry home?
Sean : No, I'm sorry. She just left for lunch.
Gloria : Could I leave a message for her?
Sean : Wait a minute. I'll get a pen.
Gloria : Okay. Please tell her that Gloria called.
Sean : No problem.
Gloria : And could you have her call me back when she has time? It's important.
Sean : I'll tell her as soon as she comes in.

Lesson.11 Describing appearance

DIALOGUE PRACTICE

Alexander : I can't find Roger. It's so crowded.
Nathan : How would you describe him?
Alexander : He's a little tall and skinny with brown hair.
Nathan : Does he have a beard?
Alexander : No, he doesn't.
Nathan : I don't know. I can't see anyone who fits the description.
Alexander : I see him now! He's the man standing over there by the ticket machine.
Nathan : I can't wait to meet him.

COMPREHENSIVE LISTENING

James : I'm waiting outside the coffee shop. I can't find Claire.
Irene : She told me she's sitting at a table in the middle.
James : How would you describe her?
Irene : She's tall and thin with long hair.
James : What color is her hair?
Irene : It's light brown and a little curly.
James : Oh! She's the one over there.
Irene : Great! You found her.

Lesson.12 Describing characteristics

DIALOGUE PRACTICE

Nora : Did you enjoy meeting Diane last night?
Jack : Yes, she's a very nice woman.
Nora : What did you think of her personality?
Jack : I'd describe her as a very friendly person.
Nora : Yes, she is a very outgoing woman. She has a bright personality.
Jack : I hope that I can meet her again soon.
Nora : I think she'll be at Harry's party next week.
Jack : Are you going, too?

COMPREHENSIVE LISTENING

Alex : Is it okay if my friend Bill joins us for dinner?
Ellen : That's no problem. What's your friend like?
Alex : My friend has an energetic personality.
Ellen : Is he very talkative?
Alex : Yes, he's a very outgoing man.
Ellen : He sounds nice.
Alex : He has a great sense of humor. I'd describe him as a very funny man.
Ellen : I can't wait to meet him tonight.

AUDIO SCRIPTS

Lesson.13   I should have…

DIALOGUE PRACTICE

Harper	:	Thank you so much for the ride.
Natalie	:	What would you have done if I hadn't been there to help?
Harper	:	I don't know. I wish I hadn't forgotten my wallet, or I would have taken a taxi.
Natalie	:	Missing the last bus was unfortunate.
Harper	:	I know. I shouldn't have waited so late.
Natalie	:	It's okay. You can call me anytime.
Harper	:	You're a really great friend.
Natalie	:	No problem. Try to leave for the bus earlier next time.

COMPREHENSIVE LISTENING

John	:	Staying home this summer was unfortunate.
Suzie	:	I know. I shouldn't have waited so late to book tickets.
John	:	It was my fault. I wish I hadn't waited so long to take off work.
Suzie	:	I think the kids still had a good time.
John	:	Yes, they seemed to enjoy staying at home.
Suzie	:	I think it's because their daddy was here.
John	:	I enjoyed it, too.
Suzie	:	Maybe it wasn't such a bad vacation.

Lesson.14   Special occasions

DIALOGUE PRACTICE

Cooper	:	You're getting married next year, right?
Samantha	:	Yes, in April.
Cooper	:	Have you picked a place to have your wedding yet?
Samantha	:	I wish I had a plan, but I don't have the time to look at anywhere.
Cooper	:	If I had the money, I'd have it in a hotel downtown.
Samantha	:	That would be nice. If I had time, I would probably look into that.
Cooper	:	What would you do if you had unlimited money for your wedding?
Samantha	:	I'd have to think about that….

COMPREHENSIVE LISTENING

Brian	:	What would you do if you had another week of vacation?
Michelle	:	If I had time, I would go on vacation somewhere.
Brian	:	Where would you want to go?
Michelle	:	If I had the money, I'd want to go to the Maldives. How about you?
Brian	:	If I had the money?
Michelle	:	Yes, where would you want to go?
Brian	:	I'd want to go to Europe.
Michelle	:	Europe sounds great too.

Lesson.15 Holiday plans

DIALOGUE PRACTICE

Sebastian : Are you planning on taking a vacation for the holidays?
Molly : No, I'm just going to hang out at home while I'm off work.
Sebastian : That sounds very restful.
Molly : What are you doing for New Year's Eve?
Sebastian : My cousin is having a big party.
Molly : That sounds fun.
Sebastian : You should come, too.
Molly : Are you sure? I'd hate to invite myself along.

COMPREHENSIVE LISTENING

Vince : What are you doing for the long weekend?
Tracey : I'm going to visit my parents while I'm off work.
Vince : Where do your parents live?
Tracey : They live in Georgetown.
Vince : That's not too far away.
Tracey : What about you? Are you planning on doing anything for the holiday?
Vince : I might have to work. I have a big presentation to work on.
Tracey : That's too bad.

Lesson.16 Getting away

DIALOGUE PRACTICE

Keira : Are you ready for your new job?
Alyssa : Yes, I'm really excited.
Keira : You aren't worried about changing careers?
Alyssa : No, I'm optimistic about the opportunity.
Keira : That's a good way to think about it.
Alyssa : Yes, I'm looking forward to doing something different.
Keira : You won't miss your students?
Alyssa : No, I'm ready to work with adults again.

COMPREHENSIVE LISTENING

Jaden : I'm looking forward to my vacation.
Hillary : Where are you going?
Jaden : I'm going hiking in the Himalayas.
Hillary : Aren't you worried it might be difficult?
Jaden : I'm optimistic about the experience. The views will be great.
Hillary : I bet you're excited.
Jaden : Yes, I'm ready to start my vacation now. I don't know if I can wait another week.
Hillary : I can't wait to hear about it when you get back.

COMMON MISTAKES

Lesson.01

Answers

1. I will let you know by tomorrow.
2. You need to finish dinner by seven.
3. The children will play soccer until it becomes dark.

Explanation

by vs. until

Both *until* and *by* indicate "any time before, but not later than."
Until tells us how long a situation continues. If something happens *until* a particular time, you stop doing it at that time.
If something happens *by* a particular time, it happens at or before that time. It is often used to indicate a deadline. *By* is also used when asking questions.

Lesson.02

Answers

1. He gave me some help.
2. They didn't have any water.
3. Could you give me some help?

Explanation

any vs. some

Any and *some* are both determiners. They are used to talk about indefinite quantities or numbers, when the exact quantity or number is not important.
Some is used for positive statements.
Any is used for questions and negative statements.
Note - You will sometimes see *some* in questions and *any* in positive statements. When making an offer, or a request, in order to encourage the person we are speaking to, to say "Yes", you can use *some* in a question. *Any* can also be used in a positive statement if it comes after a word whose meaning is negative or limiting.

Lesson.03

Answers

1. Did anyone go to the party?
2. I can recommend any one of these books.
3. Did anyone in the class finish their homework?

Explanation

any one vs. anyone

Any one means any single person or thing out of a group of people or things.
Anyone means any person. It's always written as one word.

Lesson.04

Answers

1. I like to watch a movie.
2. I can see the smoke from here.
3. I want to look at the stars.

Explanation

see vs. watch

See means to be aware of what is around you by using your eyes.
Watch means to deliberately look at something for a period of time, especially something that is changing or moving.

Note : We watch things that move, such as TV, a film, sport. We look at static things, such as a photograph, a painting, the stars.

PRE GET UP TO SPEED 2
ANSWER KEY

Lesson.05

Answers

1. When you leave, make sure you take an umbrella.
2. Can you bring some souvenirs for us?
3. When you go to the dinner party, take a bottle of wine.

Explanation

bring vs. take
When you are viewing the movement of something from the point of arrival, use *bring*.
Viewing things from the point of departure, you should use *take*.

Lesson.06

Answers

1. The camel was lost in the desert.
2. Dessert is my favorite part of the meal.
3. There is very little rainfall in the desert.

Explanation

dessert vs. desert
Dessert is a noun referring to the final course of a meal, usually a form of sweet, delicacy, or fruit.
Desert is a noun referring to a body of land with very little rainfall.

Lesson.07

Answers

1. Let's go shopping at the mall.
2. He lets his students run in the classroom.
3. The boy lets the dog sleep on the bed.

Explanation

lets vs. let's
Lets has the meaning of "allows" or "permits."
Let's is always a contraction of "let us."

Lesson.08

Answers

1. I wonder how the weather is in France.
2. Whether the boy ate the chocolate remained a mystery.
3. I'm not sure whether you will like it or not.

Explanation

weather vs. whether
Weather and *whether* are homonyms, words with different spelling and meanings but the same pronunciation.
Weather can be used either as a noun or a verb. As a noun, it refers to the climate. As a verb, it means to withstand something.
Whether is a conjunction which joins two words or phrases together. It is similar in meaning to the word "if", and links two possible choices together.

Common mistakes

COMMON MISTAKES

Lesson.09

Answers

1. I think lightening the color of your hair is a good idea.
2. The boy was afraid of the lightning.
3. Her face lightened after hearing the news.

Explanation

lightening vs. lightning

Lightening and *lightning* are homonyms, words with different spelling and meanings but the same pronunciation.
Lightening has the meaning which means that you are making something lighter. Examples include, lightening your load or the color of your hair.
Lightning is a noun which refers to the bright flashes of light during a storm.

Lesson.10

Answers

1. New York is far from London.
2. My school is 10 minutes from the shop.
3. You should take the bus, it's too far to walk.

Explanation

far

Far is mainly used in questions and negative sentences. In affirmative sentences, people usually say a *long way*.
Far is used in affirmative sentences only when it appears in phrases, such as too far, quite far, or far away.
Far cannot be used after a unit of distance. A place that is a long distance from another place is *far away*.

Lesson.11

Answers

1. I have been waiting for ten minutes.
2. She has been working in France since last winter.
3. They will visit for a week.

Explanation

for vs. since

The prepositions *for* and *since* are often used with time expressions.
For indicates a period of time.
Since indicates a point in time.

Note : Just remember this sentence "For a length of time, since a point in time."

Lesson.12

Answers

1. There is not much milk left.
2. We picked too many strawberries on the farm.
3. How many brothers do you have?

Explanation

much vs. many

Much and *many* are used to express that there is a large quantity of something. They are used in negative sentences and questions.
Many is used with countable nouns.
Much is used with uncountable nouns.

Note : we almost never use **much** and **many** in positive sentences, we almost always use "a lot of" or "lots of."

PRE GET UP TO SPEED 2
ANSWER KEY

Lesson.13

Answers

1. The waiter asked if we were all together.
2. The boy played the piano less and less and eventually stopped altogether.
3. Altogether, I have worked in this company for 15 years.

Explanation

altogether vs. all together

Altogether and *all together* are homonyms, words with different spelling and meanings but the same pronunciation.
All together is an adverb that means "together in a single group."
Altogether is an adverb that means "completely" or "in total."

Lesson.14

Answers

1. Every day I go for a run in the park.
2. Being late is an everyday event for him.
3. He wants to eat pizza every day.

Explanation

every day vs. everyday

Every day and *everyday* are homonyms, words with different spelling and meanings but the same pronunciation.
In *every day*, every is a determiner and day is a noun. When you say *every day* you mean each day without exception.
Everyday is an adjective. When you say *everyday* you mean ordinary, unremarkable.

Lesson.15

Answers

1. Playing sports makes me feel excited.
2. The children were excited to bake cookies.
3. I think that this movie is very exciting.

Explanation

excited vs. exciting

Excited is an adjective that describes when someone feels happy and enthusiastic about something.
Exciting is an adjective that means something is making you excited.

Lesson.16

Answers

1. As soon as I put on a coat, I will be all ready.
2. She was already at the restaurant.
3. They were all ready to order.

Explanation

all ready vs. already

All ready and *already* are homonyms, words with different spelling and meanings but the same pronunciation.
All ready is a phrase meaning "completely prepared."
Already is an adverb used to describe something that has happened before a certain time.

Common mistakes